Praise for *The Emotional Overdraft*

Making a profit should not mean living in debt; Andy's book gives leaders the keys to unlock SUSTAINABLE success. Leadership is about more than managing an organisation. It begins by managing yourself. This book provides practical tools for leading both a business and a life. Invest in it.

James Kerr, author of the global bestseller *Legacy*

The Emotional Overdraft is a must-read for anyone running a business. It proves that you really can grow a successful business without sacrificing your well-being.

James Hilton, Chairman of M&C Saatchi Performance

Wellbeing is a vital resource to organisations seeking to thrive. That resource is increasingly undervalued and misunderstood for leaders and managers. Andy Brown's book eloquently, effectively and evidentially rights that wrong. Essential reading for today's leaders.

Paul Levy, Author of *Digital Inferno* and Senior Research Fellow at the Centre for Research in Innovation Management, University of Brighton

A fantastic resource for leaders in SMEs to break out of stress and live a more fulfilled life in business. Enlightening and practical – every person scaling a small business needs this book.

Ruth Farenga, founder of Conscious Leaders and author of *Next Level Leadership*

Having spent a decade experiencing the highs and lows of growing my business, Andy Brown's book hit a nerve. The cost of building an 'emotional overdraft' is carried by you, your business, and those you care about. So, if you're a founder or leader feeling the strain, take some time to read his book and learn from the first-hand lessons he's acquired over twenty years. *The Emotional Overdraft* is not just a worthwhile idea, it's absolutely necessary.

Ollie Henderson, bestselling author of *Work/Life Flywheel*

The Emotional Overdraft gives the feeling of pressure you have as a leader a name, and the book makes it possible to reduce your emotional overdraft, not by learning new skills, but by changing behaviours. Having been a Global CEO of household named brands I totally appreciate where he's coming from and wish I'd had the benefit of his insight earlier in my journey.

Hugh Wahla, life purpose coach and mentor, formerly CEO at The Conran Shop and MD at Urban Outfitters

The Emotional Overdraft shines light on the real cost of our work – beyond simply the time that we take to get something done. It's a reminder to take care of ourselves, to be kind to those around us, and to remember that great work isn't scuppered or inconvenienced by 'life' and 'balance' – it's fuelled by them.

Graham Allcott, bestselling author of *How to Be a Productivity Ninja* and presenter of the 'Beyond Busy' podcast

10 simple changes
for balancing
business success
and wellbeing

the emotional overdraft

ANDY
BROWN

Contents

Introduction

IF YOU'RE A founder or leader of a people-based business, it can be a struggle to change the way you work as your company grows. Not long before I wrote this book, I attended an event for small businesses and found myself drawn into an animated discussion about people's never-ending to-do lists. One man, the owner of a management consultancy, put the problem particularly well: 'When I first started my company, I wore 12 hats – I ran around doing everything myself and dreamed of the day when I'd have staff to offload the work onto. Now I have 12 staff but I still seem to wear 12 hats. In fact, I wear more, because I've added manager and leader to the collection.' There was a lot of nodding and eye-rolling at this; clearly, he'd touched a nerve. 'It's terrible,' he continued. 'I spend all my time either working on things that other people should be doing or learning stuff that I'll probably never be good at. It's ridiculous, I know, but I can't see what else to do.'

This is the crux of the problem. Just like this man, when you found a business, you start off by wearing all the hats, that depend on people for their success need to put their own people at the centre of their decision making.

For the past seven years, I've worked as an adviser (sometimes called a non-executive director or sometimes just a friend) and coach to people-based businesses, helping them to become more valuable. During this time, I've noticed that almost everyone leading an organization is paying a hidden price that perhaps they don't, or can't, acknowledge. They seem to accept that making an impact inevitably involves a trade-off between their happiness or physical health and the success of their business. This is something that I experienced myself in the early years, a time when I worked ridiculously long hours. There were days when I'd crawl home at midnight and climb into bed next to my small children to cuddle them, crying when I thought about all the things I'd missed that day and the time I'd never get back.

Until a couple of years ago, I didn't have a name for this issue, but I started to think of it as a form of borrowing – an overdraft, if you will. My background in research and my natural curiosity led me to dig deeper to discover whether this was a universal issue. After I completed my research (which I explain in more detail in later chapters), I was astonished by the degree to which almost all leaders had this problem. I decided that I needed a name for it – a way of describing what they were doing and how it felt. With my experience in advertising, you won't be surprised to learn that I'm a believer in brands: labels that act as a shorthand for a complex mixture of attributes and that help people to recognize a concept. I came up with 'the emotional overdraft' and found that it resonated with everyone I explained it to.

I should add that, while there are qualitative and quantitative measures behind my research, it's not scientifically based. The idea of the emotional overdraft is something that I created as a result of what I've observed through years of working with, and in, people-based businesses. The measure of its potential impact on you will be if you find that it has a positive effect on your wellbeing.

So how does this book work? In Part One, we explore what an emotional overdraft is and what you can learn about your own. In Part Two, I delve more deeply into the concept and explain the 10 reasons why most leaders run up an emotional overdraft. Part Three is the big one: how to reduce or even eliminate your emotional overdraft. And in Part Four, we look at how you can take things several steps further if you want to.

Every leader I've ever worked with has the talent and ability to build a successful business. You do, too. But, just like them, you may not be asking yourself the right questions or tapping into the insights within you that are waiting to be discovered. When you do, you'll realize that reducing your emotional overdraft is not only essential for a rewarding and happy life, but also for leading a business filled with people who are working in a sustainable and productive way. Let's make a start.

Part One
The Fundamentals

1

What Is an Emotional Overdraft?

Picture the scene. It's your end-of-year financial review, and you and your team are sitting around the boardroom table. Your finance director (FD) is taking you through the figures and, overall, the news is good. After a horrendous 12 months the previous year, when you faced all sorts of challenges, you're finally back on track and it feels great to be facing the future with optimism. There's one thing troubling you, though. When you look at your profit and loss account, every single month is showing a lovely black profit figure, apart from one month when it dips slightly into the red. A voice in your head tells you that it doesn't matter – it's only the number at the end of the year that counts. But wouldn't it be nice if every month could be in profit, especially after the awful time that you've had? You could all do with a boost. Everyone around the table agrees, and your FD says that all that's needed is to shuffle a couple of sales into the affected month and, hey presto, you're in profit for each month of the year. He even does it in front of you as he speaks. This is fantastic! Everyone in the room gives a whoop and a cheer, and you promise to celebrate in suitable style that very afternoon.

As any business owner will tell you, that profitability figure at the bottom right of the profit and loss statement (P&L) is important. It's the measure of your success, so why shouldn't you create an artificial morale-booster by rearranging the figures to make them look more satisfying? No real harm has been done. However, there's another way that you may be 'fiddling the figures', and it's one that you're probably not aware of; worst of all, it's insidious. It's when you subsidize your business's profitability at the expense of your own mental and physical health.

It's easiest to understand this through an example scenario – the kind of thing that happens in many of the businesses I work with. Suppose you're the founder of a firm that's winning more and more clients, and you need to recruit a new team member to manage the extra load. The problem is, good staff are hard to find, and you can't seem to attract the right person; three months into your recruitment search, you're still drawing a blank. The rest of your team is already maxed out, so, while you already have a lot on your plate, there seems no option but for you to handle the new clients yourself. You work long hours over those months while you somehow juggle everything that needs to be done. You cancel the strategic planning session that you've been meaning to hold for weeks, and the supplier review that you know you should be getting on with. It worries you that you're not attending to those important areas of the business but you plough on because you feel you have no choice. Your stress levels are high, leading you to become impatient with your team, miss an important doctor's appointment and snap at your kids for leaving the house in a mess when you finally arrive home at 9:00 pm.

There's one consolation, though, which is your figures. You'd allocated £4000 a month in salary costs for the yet-to-be-recruited staff member, and because you still haven't found them three months on, you're £12,000 more in the black than you would have been otherwise. Result! However, let's pause for a moment. Is your business really better off? You originally decided you needed to hire a new person for a reason, which was that everyone was too stretched. Could there be a hidden cost line in your P&L? One that represents the personal price you paid when you took on the client work yourself? Imagine if it were possible to put a number on that cost, just like you can with your marketing costs or travel expenses. Would your company still be in profit, or would you be staring at a big, fat loss?

The emotional overdraft

When you overcome your business challenges at the expense of your own mental and physical health, you're effectively subsidizing it with an emotional overdraft. You're dipping into your personal reserves to keep the company going, and if you do it for too long, you eventually run out of credit.

Of course, sometimes it's necessary to get into 'debt' – overdraft facilities are there to help us when we need them. When I ran an advertising agency, pitching for new business always left me drawing hard on my emotional overdraft. As well as my normal workload, I had to spend a lot of time preparing a proposal and presentation for the potential client; I worked long hours, neglecting my family and using every ounce of energy I had to push through. After it was over, I and the rest of the pitch team would celebrate a job well done and work would go back to normal. My overdraft would be paid off. The point is that it's emotionally sustainable to burst through into your overdraft on occasion; the problem comes when you live in your overdraft all the time. As any finance expert will tell you, an overdraft is an expensive way to borrow – it's not designed for long-term use. You have to pay it back as quickly as you can or risk being overwhelmed by the pressure.

Going back to the P&L that I talked about earlier, the figure at the bottom right should be the *consequence* of all the things that you've done well (or badly) in your business over the year. If you ignore your own emotional subsidy, you're effectively massaging that number so that it shows what you want to see. The result is that it's not a real profit figure, it's a contorted one that you've manufactured to convince yourself that your business is more successful than it actually is.

The resilience factor

The currency you use when you dip into your emotional overdraft is your resilience. This, as educational leadership expert Dr Janet Ledesma says, is 'the ability to bounce back from adversity, frustration and misfortune'.[1] We all have different levels of resilience; some leaders are amazingly well supplied with it, even when they're dealing with the toughest of challenges; it's as if they're almost superhuman. However, it's not a good idea to compare yourself to others. Just as some people feel relatively relaxed about getting into debt, so some people can cope with stress and pressure more easily than their peers. Also, you don't even know whether what you're comparing yourself to is real. We've all seen the social media posts: 'I get up at 5:00 am to work out before I start my day'; 'I smashed my targets for this month in week one'; 'I'll make a million a year'. These are often a front created by a person who is, in reality, struggling as much as you may be.

So, resilience isn't something that you should be competitive about, but it is a crucial factor in your wellbeing and, as such, you need to understand it. In her article 'How Resilience Works', Diane Coutu examines many theories about resilience and identifies that resilient people possess three common characteristics: 'a staunch acceptance of reality; a deep belief, often buttressed by strongly held values, that life is meaningful; and an uncanny ability to improvise'.[2] Considering the first characteristic in more

---

[1] Janet Ledesma, *Narratives of Longevity from the Perspective of Seventh-day Adventist School Administrators in North America: A Multiple Case Study*, PhD diss., Andrews University, Michigan (2011).

[2] Diane Coutu, 'How Resilience Works', *Harvard Business Review*, May (2002). Available at: https://hbr.org/2002/05/how-resilience-works [accessed 29 July 2023].

detail, the idea that we need to accept reality if we're to be resilient seems fundamental to me, and is explored further by Jim Collins in his book *Good to Great*. In this, he tells the tale of Admiral John Stockdale, who was held captive for eight years during the Vietnam War. He was tortured over 20 times and, despite having no release date and no idea if or when he would see his family again, he managed to devise ingenious and courageous ways for both him and the other prisoners to survive. When Collins asks him who the people were who *didn't* make it out of the camps, Stockdale replied, 'Oh, that's easy. The optimists.' They were the captives who kept thinking that they'd be out by Christmas, and when they weren't, in Stockdale's words, they ended up dying 'of a broken heart'.[3]

Admiral Stockdale may seem like a tough act to follow but, as I'm sure you'll have experienced, having a high level of resilience is essential when you're running a business. Just as an overdraft facility has a limit, so your supply of the currency of resilience is finite; when you constantly work at your own emotional expense, you run up a debt. The most dangerous thing about this is that it's easy to think you can handle it through optimism: 'I just need to get through this week and then I can relax.' Or: 'We have to man-up and muscle through the problem – let's go for it!' And if it *is* only short term, that's manageable. But when you're regularly drawing on your reserves of resilience without replenishing them, eventually they run dry and you can find yourself unable to recover from even the smallest of

---

[3] Jim Collins, *Good to Great: Why Some Companies Make the Leap… and Others Don't*, Harper Business (2001), pp. 83–85.

difficulties. That's when, at the extreme end of the scale, you find yourself unable to get out of bed in the morning or make a simple decision.

Fortunately, resilience is a skill that you can learn. As Diane Coutu says, 'Resilience is neither ethically good or bad. It's merely the skill and the capacity to be robust under conditions of stress or change.'[4] In practice, it involves making the most of what you have, being inventive and using familiar things in unfamiliar ways. Instead of thinking 'Why me?' resilient people think, 'Why not me? What can I learn from this? What can I do to adapt to the situation?' They're not blindly optimistic but focus instead on constructing meaning from their difficult circumstances. They use the hardship they're experiencing to build bridges to a better future, and this reduces their feelings of overwhelm and stress. These are approaches that you can practice, and which you'll discover ways of fostering in this book.

Compound interest on your emotional overdraft

I once worked with a client, Scott, who'd originally founded his company with a business partner. The relationship between the two men was deteriorating, so Scott was debating with himself whether he should leave the business or stay on and buy his partner out. He found himself going round in circles, unable to decide what to do, until we spoke.

---

[4] Diane Coutu, 'How Resilience Works', *Harvard Business Review*, May (2022). Available at: https://hbr.org/2002/05/how-resilience-works [accessed 26 September 2023].

What I was able to show him was that it wasn't the decision-making process that was causing the struggle, but the mental distraction of it. Scott was, in effect, creating problems out of thin air in addition to the 'real' one that he had, and this in turn was impacting his resilience.

That's how our brains often work: we have an issue to deal with, but instead of just focusing on that issue we create extra thoughts about it that turn it into a bigger one. Let's return to my example scenario of throwing yourself into new client work and neglecting important strategic areas of the business. You're not stupid – you know what you're doing and it's stressing you out. Your staff are depending on you to help them deliver for clients, but they're depending on you just as much to win more work in the future and to run a business that makes a profit. There's a tape playing in your head on a continuous loop: 'I've got to involve myself with the clients, but I should be doing these other things instead. It's what I'm here for – I'm the leader. But I have to do the client work, so what can I do? I can't just expect the team to do it all.' And on it goes.

It's as if your thoughts are the interest that's being added to your emotional overdraft, increasing it day by day until it's stretched to the limit. This means that your resilience – your ability to overcome challenges and bounce back from difficulties – is greatly reduced. Adding to your stress by thinking of all the negative implications of your impossible situation is a perfectly normal thing to do, but it's a horrible mental state to be in and is another way in which emotional overdrafts are run up.

Other people's emotional overdrafts

It probably won't surprise you to learn that if you have the capacity to run up an emotional overdraft, so does everyone else in your life and work. Your colleagues, your family, your friends – all of them have their own resilience levels to manage, and your actions can have a direct impact on how well they're able to do that.

From a business perspective, this can have consequences. Suppose you're going through a particularly stretching period at work. One morning, you arrive early to tackle your backlog of emails and check your calendar for the day. There's a review meeting with your marketing manager scheduled for 11:00 am. You haven't got time for that – today is for urgent stuff only – so, feeling guilty because it's the second time you've done it, you reschedule for next month. This relieves the immediate pressure, but what happens when your marketing manager receives the news that the review they've been preparing for has been put back? How do they feel? Like a valued member of your team? As someone worthy of consideration? They might have been planning to discuss their career aspirations or talk to you about the training they need, but now that opportunity has been taken away from them. Again.

If you're regularly subsidizing your business by taking on responsibilities that, as a leader, you shouldn't be burdening yourself with, you'll almost certainly be having an impact on other people's mental wellbeing as well as your own. Your employees won't be receiving the training and support they need, so they'll just carry on doing the best they can without it. In the end, the weaker members of staff will stay but the stronger ones will leave. They'll say to themselves: 'I have lots of ideas but no one ever listens to them, I'm getting no training, and this job seems like it's going nowhere. The next call I get from a headhunter, I'll take it.'

Then what happens, horrendously, is that staff leave and a raft of new problems emerge. Who's going to pick up the work? You're now going to become involved in even more activities that you should be staying away from, increasing your emotional overdraft to potentially unsustainable levels. This is how overdrafts get racked up: it's rarely one challenge on its own, it's an insidious build-up of issue after issue which adds up to a hefty emotional debt.

There are also your relationships outside work to consider. When you overload yourself at work, you probably find yourself drawing on that person's emotional reserves, maybe without realizing it. If you don't spend much time with your loved ones and you're not a great person to be around when you do, you're relying on their overdraft facility to subsidize yours. If you borrow from it for long enough, eventually those people will run out of credit to supply you with.

It's easy to do – I've spoken with many former entrepreneurs who were, at the time, in a state of denial about the impact they were having on other people's overdrafts. It's only when they look back on their lives that they realize what a toll it took on their families and friends. Separation, being estranged from their children, losing friendships and missing out on the things that they wanted to do outside of work when they were in the prime of their lives – these are all manifestations of an unsustainable emotional overdraft. It's fine to want to achieve business success, but it's also a good idea to ask yourself if it's being 'funded' by other people's emotional wellbeing.

The value of human capital

One of the reasons that it's easy to ignore the invisible line in the P&L – the figure that represents the emotional cost to you and your team of delivering the final profit – is that it's difficult to quantify. Thankfully, there are increasing numbers of experts who are examining the value of what they call 'human capital', or employees' talent, skills, personal attributes and creativity. As a report from the International Integrated Reporting Council says, 'Understanding the links between human capital and organizational outcomes brings benefits.... It can fill an information gap, providing valuable insights... on an organization's potential to succeed over the short, medium and long term.'[5]

At the heart of all the research I've read exploring the link between people's performance at work and the profitability of their organizations lies the fact that the better you lead people, the more successful the business will be. The Chartered Institute of Personnel and Development notes that, '... poor people management and inadequate training

---

[5] Integrated Reporting, *Creating Value: The Value of Human Capital Reporting*. Report from the International Integrated Reporting Council (IIRC) (2015), p. 4. Available at: www. integratedreporting.org/wp-content/uploads/2017/05/ CreatingValueHumanCapitalK1.pdf [accessed 16 August 2023].

are now widely recognized as having played significant roles in numerous corporate failures over the last 10 years.'[6] And, more positively, research and advisory firm Creelman Lambert & McBassi states in its *Smarter Annual Report* that, 'At the heart of value creation lie factors such as quality and stability of leadership, depth of talent, innovation and employee brand.'[7]

This is important because, in the business world, financial measures have traditionally been the only ones that are highlighted. So, it's refreshing to see that workforce health metrics are now considered to be an important indicator of how well a company is doing. Part of this should surely be the levels of resilience within each of its employees, which are in turn created by how small or large their emotional overdrafts are. We'll come to how you can quantify your emotional overdraft in a bit.

I hope you don't feel overwhelmed by the scale of the issue I've presented here. I've deliberately been heavy-hitting because I want to wake you up to the problem – otherwise, it's easy to ignore it until it becomes a crisis. However, there

---

[6] Chartered Institute of Personnel and Development (CIPD), *Human Capital Reporting: Investing for Sustainable Growth* (2015). Available at: www.integratedreporting.org/wp-content/uploads/2017/05/CreatingValueHumanCapitalK1.pdf, p. 8 [accessed 16 August 2023].

[7] Creelman Lambert & McBassi, *The Smarter Annual Report: How Companies Are Integrating Financial and Human Capital Reporting* (2014). Available at: https://creelmanlambert.files.wordpress.com/2013/01/the_smarter_annual_report-full-colour.pdf [accessed 26 September 2023].

is good news. Just as quickly as your emotional overdraft can increase to breaking point, so it can also correct itself, because there are ways of running a business that *don't* involve you taking everything upon yourself. Resilient companies aren't managed like that because their leaders don't see running up a long-term emotional overdraft as an inevitable part of doing their job. This can apply to you, too, and it's what the rest of this book will help you with.

In the next chapter, you'll discover the size of your own emotional overdraft.

The bottom line

- When you overcome your business challenges at the expense of your own mental and physical health, you effectively subsidize your company with an emotional overdraft.

- A healthy leader uses their emotional overdraft to increase their impact when it's needed, but then clears it.

- The currency you spend when you increase your emotional overdraft is your resilience.

- Adding to your stress by obsessing over the negative implications of your impossible situation is like adding compound interest to your emotional overdraft.

- Other people have emotional overdrafts as well, so you need to be careful not to draw too heavily on their reserves.

2

Do You Have an Emotional Overdraft?

THE FIRST STEP in addressing a problem is to acknowledge that it exists. You're almost certainly carrying some level of emotional overdraft, but here's where you can find out for sure. You'll also learn how big it is and where it shows up most often in your life.

Some of the questions, or the scoring, may give you pause or feel slightly curious. These questions start to explore the specific behaviours that are driving your emotional overdraft. The reasons for these questions will become apparent later in this chapter and as you work through the book.

Answer the following questions relating to how you think about your business. I don't expect that you'll feel the same way about each question every day, so simply give yourself two points if it applies to you *some or all* of the time, and one point if it *rarely or never* does. Try not to overthink the process; it shouldn't take you more than a few minutes.

An online version of this self-assessment tool is also available at www.emotionaloverdraft.com. This calculates your score for you and gives you a personalized 'Emotional Overdraft Profile', which you can download and use however you want. You can even download the tool so that you can complete it offline. However, if you don't have a device to hand or if you prefer the pen and paper approach, you can fill in the answers manually on the list below.

A reminder: give yourself two points if a question applies to you some or all of the time, and one point if it rarely or never does.

Question	Statement	Score
1	I put work before family.	
2	We seem to over service our clients.	
3	It's easier for me to be flexible with time than it is for my colleagues.	
4	I consider myself to be a nice person.	
5	My to-do list is endless.	
6	I worry that I don't have enough time for my family.	
7	Clients and customers are impossible to satisfy.	
8	I have the technical knowledge to help out my teams.	
9	I find it hard to tell my staff what I'm really thinking.	

10	I find myself getting frustrated with my team.	
11	The buck stops with me.	
12	When my team is stretched, I step in.	
13	It's quicker to do it than explain it.	
14	I won't let a colleague struggle.	
15	I see myself as a 'doer'.	
16	I'm the boss so I have to accept the pressure.	
17	When others are overwhelmed, I step in.	
18	I could do with a few more staff.	
19	I feel closely connected to my team.	
20	I love ticking tasks off a to-do list.	
21	I don't have a written job description.	
22	Our processes could be better.	
23	I agree to do other people's tasks even if my own work might suffer.	
24	I feel responsible for the success of my team.	
25	I may not be the best at prioritizing.	
26	Friends ask me why I work such long hours.	
27	Recruiting the right people is stressful.	
28	I worry that our competitors are one step ahead of us.	
29	People let me down.	
30	I'd like more time for my hobbies and passions.	

31	Firefighting is just part of the job.	
32	I worry about cashflow and late payers.	
33	I've kept staff on for longer than I should.	
34	I'm the escalation point.	
35	I resent having to work.	
36	I roll up my sleeves and pitch in when my staff are struggling.	
37	I hesitate to make new hires even if we need them.	
38	The important people in my life get annoyed when I work long hours.	
39	Delegation doesn't come naturally to me.	
40	Difficult clients are my problem to solve.	
41	I accept stress as part of my job.	
42	I find it hard to charge what we're worth.	
43	I feel like I'm in catch-up mode.	
44	Having staff working remotely worries me.	
45	I'm able to do most jobs in my company.	
46	I don't receive support from a coach or adviser.	
47	Keeping costs down puts me under pressure.	
48	I'd love to have more people who could give me advice and support.	
49	My business is my baby.	
50	I can't always rely on my senior management team to deal with problems.	

How did you do?

Add up your answers and put the total here: _____.
Then use your score to choose the most appropriate evaluation below.

76–100: You have an ever-present emotional overdraft

You're carrying around the weight of an emotional overdraft in an ever-present way. It's having a significant impact on your personal life, your relationships at work and the success of your business. You probably think you don't have a choice about this – that it's just the way things are when you run a business. You're wrong. It's never too late to clear an emotional overdraft and you can start to reduce yours today. If you've used the online tool, you'll be aware of your most vulnerable areas and you can prioritize the chapters in this book that focus on them. Good luck – you've already started to make things better for your mental and physical health.

61–75: Your emotional overdraft is limiting you

You have an emotional overdraft, and it's not only affecting your resilience but also limiting the positive impact you could be having on your business. However, it's not overwhelming you most of the time. Your mission is to ensure that it doesn't become a constant drain on your emotional resources and to find ways of reducing it. By taking note of the areas in which your resilience is most vulnerable, and focusing your attention on the chapters in this book that are most relevant to you, you can build on what you're already doing well.

50–60: You are tuned-in to your emotional overdraft

You have an occasional emotional overdraft, but it's under control and you don't let it rule your life. This is great news. However, there are always alternative ways to run your business, so please explore the rest of the book with a curious mind. If you get forensic with your understanding of where you rely on your emotional overdraft, who knows what you could achieve? Another thing to consider is that being able to cope so well with the challenges of running a business means that you might not be aware of the emotional overdrafts that other people are carrying. It's important that you're not inadvertently drawing on their reserves to bolster your own, and that you're able to relate to why your colleagues and family may feel less resilient than you at times. What you'll learn in the following chapters will help you to tune into their emotional overdrafts so that you can help them to deal with them.

If you've used the online quiz, you'll see from your personalized profile that your scores are higher in some areas than others; for instance, you might score high for 'duty' but low for 'cost'. What do these labels mean? They're the drivers for an emotional overdraft – the attitudes and assumptions that cause you to work in ways that lower your resilience levels and feel stressed. You can see a visual representation of them in Figure 1.

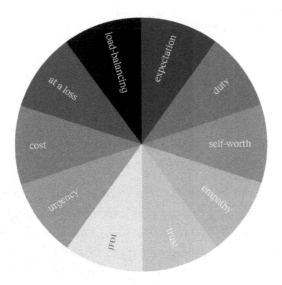

Figure 1   The emotional overdraft drivers

I'm not going to go into more detail here, as Chapters 7 to 16 will explore each driver in turn. You'll find your profile useful when you get to that point because it will help you decide where to focus your attention.

But hang on...

What did you think when you read your assessment above? Whenever I first raise the subject of the emotional overdraft with my clients, I receive a variety of responses, but they tend to run along similar lines:

- Of course I'm stressed, I run a company!

- Why wouldn't I help my teams when they're struggling? What kind of leader would I be if I turned my back on them?

- Unexpected problems always crop up – it's not realistic to think that everything will run smoothly all the time.

- Clients and customers are the lifeblood of our business. I take pride in giving them excellent service and would never resort to half measures.

These reactions are understandable because somehow, over the years, we've been programmed to assume that being a leader is inherently stressful; that we're bad people if we don't help our staff when they're struggling; that last-minute emergencies are a constant inevitability; and that we should always bend over backwards to serve our clients. The problem with this way of thinking is that it involves you drawing deeply on your emotional reserves, which in turn erodes your resilience. When you have low resilience, you're less able to deal with difficulties and challenges, and it becomes a vicious cycle of stress leading to inability to cope with stress, leading to more stress, and so on.

My request to you – just for now – is to be open to the idea that there are ways of leading a business which don't involve you operating in a permanently overdrawn state. For instance, they might involve you managing your teams in a manner that doesn't require you to step in and firefight on a regular basis, although it might be necessary on occasion. Or they could involve you seeing that intermittent periods of overwork and stress are manageable, but only if they don't happen too often and you take care to pay back your emotional overdraft afterwards.

This shift can happen more quickly than you think. When I was a kid, my dad used to drive us around in a Volvo which had one of those old-fashioned petrol gauges that used a stick in the tank. When the dashboard showed that the tank was half empty, my dad would always start looking for the nearest petrol station because he knew that the tank was a funny shape and that it was in fact almost drained of fuel. Just like that tank, our emotional reserves aren't contained in a neat box that is easy to see or quantify. Some days we're more resilient than others and, depending on what's happening around us, we can find our emotional overdrafts going up and down in an inconsistent way. The key thing is that, overall, you reduce your overdraft to manageable levels and, in the long run, learn how to exist in a debt-free state for the vast majority of the time.

Please be aware that this self-assessment is only an overview; it's designed to get you thinking about the specifics of what's causing your emotional overdraft and not (at this point) what you can do about it. If you find yourself saying, 'Yeah, I know all this anyway', keep reading because you'll learn a lot of things that will help you to feel happier and lead your business more effectively.

In the next chapter, we'll explore what emotions are and how they're not always quite what they seem.

The bottom line

- Taking steps to remove your emotional overdraft starts with acknowledging the size of it and the main drivers for it.

- Be open to the idea that having an emotional overdraft isn't an inevitable consequence of being a business leader.

- The size of your emotional overdraft can fluctuate in a way that isn't always easy to predict.

Part Two
Understanding the Emotional Overdraft

3

What Are Emotions, Anyway?

WHAT ARE EMOTIONS? It might seem like a strange question to ask, but when we talk about emotions, what do we really mean? If I was to ask you what the five senses are, you could no doubt tell me: taste, touch, smell, sight and hearing. But with emotions, there's far less clarity, and different experts have varying opinions on the matter.

The Conscious Leadership Group,[8] which helps people to understand the role of emotion in leadership, says that there are five core emotions:

- Anger

---

[8] Conscious Leadership Group, Emotional Intelligence. Available at: https://conscious.is/concepts/emotional-intelligence-resources [accessed 29 July 2023].

- Sadness

- Fear

- Joy

- Sexual feeling

However, in his theory of emotions, which he developed back in 1962, psychologist Silvan Tomkins came up with nine:[9]

- Distress

- Fear

- Anger

- Shame

- Dissmell (the characteristic way in which we react to bad odours)

- Disgust

- Interest

- Enjoyment

- Surprise

---

[9] Available at: www..tomkins.org/what-tomkins-said/introduction/nine-affects-present-at-birth-combine-to-form-emotion-mood-and-personality/ [accessed 31 July 2023].

Carroll Izard, from the University of Delaware, identified 10 primary and discrete emotions:[10]

- Fear

- Anger

- Shame

- Contempt

- Disgust

- Guilt

- Distress

- Interest

- Surprise

- Joy

And Brené Brown, in her 2021 book *Atlas of The Heart*, gives a list of 87 emotions and experiences;[11] it seems that no one can agree on how many there are and what they're called. However, that's not my point. Take another look at the three lists above and see if there's anything that stands out to you. If you're on the ball, you'll notice that there are

---

[10] Carroll E. Izard, *Human Emotions*, Springer (1977), p. 64. doi:10.1007/978-1-4899-2209-0. See also: https://en.wikipedia.org/wiki/Carroll_Izard [accessed 31 July 2023].

[11] You can download a pdf of them here: https://brenebrown.com/resources/atlas-of-the-heart-list-of-emotions/ [accessed 29 July 2023].

many more negative emotions than positive ones – around twice as many, in fact.[12]

Negative versus positive

Negative emotions have helped us survive. There's a reason for this, which is that we're hardwired to pay attention to, and learn from, negative experiences. Back in prehistoric times, when our lives were almost completely geared towards survival, we learned that if we lit a fire in our cave, the local sabre-toothed tiger would be deterred from paying a visit. If we let the fire go out, however, we soon discovered our mistake. Seeking out negative emotions was a matter of life and death; no wonder we have so many of them in relation to positive ones.

Clearly, this strategy has helped the human race to survive over the millennia. However, the legacy it's left us with is that we tend to pay a lot of attention to bad feelings but not the good ones. What effect would it have on us if we were to become more conscious of positive emotions by recognizing and celebrating them when they happened? The currency that repays our emotional overdrafts – our resilience – is fuelled by joy, interest and enjoyment. When we feel grateful for what's going well, calm about things we can't control and happy about the luck we have or the great results we achieve in life, we can deal with the ups and downs of business far more easily.

---

[12] I deliberately ordered the lists with negative first and positive second to make it easier for you, with apologies to the originators of the lists if this isn't what they intended.

The challenge with putting this into practice is that we're so stuck in our 'avoid danger at all costs' mindset that we find it hard even to *recognize* when we're having a positive experience, let alone celebrate it. Imagine that you've been working for months to win an important new client. Even before you've discovered whether or not you've been successful, you're already planning how you're going to handle the workload. Then, when the email arrives announcing that you've won, you run past the moment. 'Yay! We've done it! Amazing work, everybody,' you say. 'Right, let's get together tomorrow morning to work out how we're going to resource this. Sarah, how much have you got on right now? Tom, are you almost finished on that project? Simon, can you pull together some figures and we can take a view on the financials? Let's see how we can do this.' This is survival thinking, and while it's difficult to resist, it's far from impossible.

We have to actively seek out the positive and celebrate good news. I once worked with a brilliant advertising agency whose founders had a mission to hire only the most amazing people. For this to happen, they knew that they had to build a business that did incredible work and was renowned for nurturing its employees' talents and skills. They promised themselves that the first time someone approached them and said, 'I hear you do wonderful things and I'd love you to hire me', they would shut up shop and go to the pub to celebrate. One day, two years into their venture, someone did knock on their door and said just that. After inviting the person in for an interview, they canned all the company's meetings for the afternoon and took their 25 staff over the road for drinks. That's the difference between running past a positive emotion and recognizing it in the moment and celebrating it. Their business eventually grew to 500 employees and became incredibly successful, winning multiple awards and working with some of the biggest brands in the world. Much of this was down to the founders recognizing those joyful moments whenever they arose.

This has to be a deliberate act because the human race has spent so many thousands of years sidelining positive emotions from its consciousness. It's even more challenging to do this when you're in a state of emotional overdraft because that's when the gremlins enter your head, making you criticize yourself, focus on stressful things and worry about everything. So, the next time a good experience comes your way, grasp it with both hands and squeeze all the juice out of it that you can. Don't be careless with it. You'll sure as hell spend time dwelling on your negative emotions without the need to be asked, so at least give the positive ones some time.

As well as making sure we mark the positive times, we can make deliberate space for positive emotions by taking time out. It might be a week's holiday or an hour of swimming at the local pool. The word that gets used for this 'positive emotion bombing' is recharging. But what else is recharging – a walk in nature, time with the dog, an afternoon with a book – but a full-on grab of positive emotions? Recharging is an essential way of making time for positive emotion.

The huge importance of recharging is not just in helping us give pre-eminence to our positive emotions, it also has a great role in our ability to stay resilient. This has been shown time and time again. Shawn Achor and Michelle Gielan, in their article 'Resilience Is About How You Recharge, Not How You Endure', see recovery as being at the heart of resilience. 'The key to resilience is trying really hard, then stopping, recovering, and then trying again.' They conclude that, 'The value of a recovery period rises in proportion to the amount of work required of us.'[13] It's so obvious when you think about it – we have to stop sometimes if we're to recharge. Time and again I speak to founders and leaders who tell me that they don't have time to take a break. They move a meeting to lunchtime, they skip the gym, they defer going for a walk and having some fresh air. They do this day after day. But we're like electric cars – we need to recharge if we're to carry on moving forwards; gritting our teeth and pushing on through really is a nonsensical strategy. Recharging is how we become more resilient so that we can achieve more.

All of this leads me to conclude that we must all actively try to recognize and embrace our positive emotions and in doing so emerge from survival mode. To make that possible, we must take the time to mark and celebrate good things and make time for positive emotions by taking time out to recharge. An added bonus is that as well as

---

[13] Shawn Achor and Michelle Gielan, 'Resilience Is About How You Recharge, Not How You Endure', *Harvard Business Review*, 24 June (2016). Available at: https://hbr.org/2016/06/resilience-is-about-how-you-recharge-not-how-you-endure [accessed 29 July 2023].

countering the survival instinct, doing this will add to our resilience reservoir.

Where emotions really come from

When we understand where our emotions come from (here's a clue – they come from our own thinking), we can start to take back control.

Our prehistoric mental programming is one of the reasons we pay attention to negative emotions rather than positive, but there's also another important one – and it is to do with where our emotions come from. To explain what I mean, I'd like you to carry out a brief thought experiment.

Picture Gregory going into the office on a wet Tuesday morning after an argument with his kids over breakfast and he's glumly reading through his to-do list for the day. His heart sinks even lower than it already was. There's way too much to get through, and he knows deep down that no matter how much he wants to do everything he'll be going home that night feeling like a failure. Why does this always happen? Why can't he have one single day that feels easy? Sometimes, it doesn't feel worth it.

That's Tuesday. On Wednesday Gregory strolls into the office after a lovely walk in the sunshine and faces pretty much the same length to-do list as he did the day before. However, instead of feeling stressed and dejected, he's looking forward to attacking it with relish. The tasks are all ones that will move the business forward, and some of them have been hanging around for a long time. It will feel great to get them ticked off. Buzzing with energy, Gregory starts work straight away and blasts through the first five items before lunch.

The to-do lists are the same length and nature, but he has completely different feelings about them. Why the variation?

It comes down to his thinking. On Tuesday Gregory thought negatively about his workload but on Wednesday he felt positive about it, and those thoughts created his emotions. If it was the to-do list that was triggering his feelings, he would *always* feel the same way about it, but – as I'm sure you've personally experienced – this is not how the mind works. Your thinking creates your emotions, and your emotions create your behaviour. When you think positive thoughts, you're likely to feel happy and your subsequent behaviour reflects it; the same process is true if the thoughts are negative, but with different emotions and behaviour following on.

Thinking ⟶ Emotions ⟶ Behaviour

There's a whole philosophy around this fundamental truth about the way we experience emotions, and it's called the 'three principles'. I won't go into it here as there are many books you can read about it if you're interested,[14] but it's something that's been informing my work for a while. As three principles coach Rena Loizou once said to me: 'Your feelings are a measure of the quality of your thinking.' So, if I experience frustration, anger or sadness, the clue to why I'm feeling that way lies in the sub-optimal thoughts I'm

---

[14] I'm a fan of Michael Neill's *The Inside-Out Revolution*, Hay House (2013) – it's a three principles primer.

having. These are the things that determine my feelings, which in turn dictate my behaviour and the outcomes I get.

How does knowing this help? Because the simple act of recognizing that it's the quality of your thinking that creates your emotions means that you have an opportunity to think different thoughts – ones that are more calming or pleasurable than those which are creating the distress. Suppose one of your team lets you down yet again – how annoying. You have to do their work for them, which is frustrating and stressful enough in itself. But wait a moment: you can name your feeling of frustration and recognize that, while it *seems* as if it's caused by your employee, it's actually generated by the thoughts you have about them. Yes, it's clearly a problematic situation and one that you need to prevent happening again, but simply recognizing where the emotion comes from can immediately reduce its power. Then, you're more likely to react calmly to the issue and deal with it constructively rather than losing your cool.

Knowledge of the three principles enables us to reflect on why we react the way we do. I'm sure that you can recognize all the emotions in the lists I've given you, but you don't have to surrender to them every time. Sometimes I hear people say, 'They made me lose my temper' or, 'I get so frustrated by their behaviour'. It's only their own minds that are creating those thoughts. By naming a feeling and recognizing that it comes from you, and not the situation, makes it more manageable. You can choose to see the situation differently – to think differently about it. And this will change your emotions automatically.

Focusing on understanding what emotions are, how they work, and how they relate to our thinking and our behaviour is especially timely given the increased recognition of what's now being called the 'emotional labour' of being a leader.[15] When I talk to people about this, I find that they have an instinctive understanding of what it means. It's the expectation that you should always appear upbeat and confident in front of your teams, lest they detect the worry and uncertainty that you really feel. Or the idea that you must be an empathetic leader and cater to your employees' emotional needs, whether you want to or not. If you've ever had someone ask you for time off at short notice and felt the pressure to say, 'Of course! Is everything all right at home?' rather than, 'Oh not now, Dave, it's the worst possible time for that', you'll know what I mean.

Of course, social expectations have long dictated that female leaders carry out emotional labour, without it ever being recognized as a source of burnout; it's ironic that it's only now, when male leaders are increasingly being expected to take on this work, that it's seen as an issue. Nevertheless, an issue it is, and it's important that you recognize the toll that emotional labour can take. This is something that you'll learn more about in the next chapter where we look at the eight situations in which you're most likely to run up an emotional overdraft.

---

[15] Dina Denham Smith and Alicia A. Grandey, 'The Emotional Labor of Being a Leader', *Harvard Business Review*, 2 November (2022). Available at: https//hbr.org/2022/11/the emotional-labor-of-being-a-leader [accessed 29 July 2023].

This chapter contains a summary of two of the most valuable gifts you can give yourself. One is to consciously acknowledge the positive events that happen in your life and work, rather than only focusing on the negative. The other is to understand that all of your emotions (yes, all of them) are created by your thinking, and that by understanding where your feelings come from you can reduce the hold they have over you. Of course, if the emotions are good, feel free to immerse yourself in them as much as you like!

The bottom line

- We have names for around twice as many negative emotions as positive ones.

- Recognizing and celebrating positive emotions is an important way of reducing your emotional overdraft and strengthening your resilience.

- Our thoughts, rather than our circumstances, create our feelings, which in turn dictate our behaviour.

- Emotional labour is an increasingly recognized factor in the running up of an emotional overdraft.

4
Why You Run Up an Emotional Overdraft

FOR MANY YEARS, an important question kept bugging me. Why were the intelligent, successful and well-informed leaders who I was coaching making decisions that were costing them their resilience? Why weren't they able to see that the solutions they habitually came up with were causing them – and their organizations – harm? I knew the superficial answer: because they're human. We none of us make the ideal choice every time; instead, we tend to fall back on our ingrained thinking patterns and leap to whatever option seems most obvious.

But this wasn't enough for me. I felt a desire to dig deeper and understand what was stopping people from making better decisions – ones that would allow them to keep their mental health intact and their businesses to flourish. So, using my background in market research, I surveyed a number of business leaders in people-based, service-led firms. They comprised men and women aged from 20 to 60, with half of them being in their mid-thirties or forties. Most ran companies with turnovers ranging from £1 million to £10 million and employed between 10 and 60 staff. If this is similar to you and your business, that's great, but even if it's not, what I learnt will apply to you regardless.

I asked my research subjects two deceptively simple questions:

1. In what sorts of circumstances do you draw on your emotional reserves when there might have been an alternative?
2. Why did you choose to draw on your emotional reserves rather than find a different solution?

The answers I received told me that I was definitely on to something. Of the respondents, 91% agreed that they had paid an emotional cost to achieve an objective when it seemed simpler than finding an alternative. And 97% were of the opinion that they had usually or sometimes supported their business at the cost of their own emotional and mental health.[16] Once I had the responses to the questions recorded, I grouped them into categories to make them easier to analyze.

---

[16] Of the respondents, 45% said 'usually' and 52% said 'sometimes'.

The eight situations in which leaders run up an emotional overdraft

In answer to the first question (*'In what sort of circumstances do you draw on your emotional reserves when there might have been an alternative?'*), I identified eight categories of situation in which my respondents had been prepared to dip into their emotional reserves.

1. When the team was under pressure and they put team needs ahead of their own.
2. When dealing with people and HR issues.
3. When they believed that they were the only person who could do something or didn't trust anyone else to do it.
4. In urgent situations or when time was tight.
5. When dealing with new ideas, clients or services.
6. When family and friends seemed less important than work.
7. When money was tight or they lacked resources.
8. When trying to be kind.

Do you recognize some or all of these circumstances, even if they relate to other people's behaviour rather than your own? I certainly recognize them in myself. Of course, they're not mutually exclusive; it's possible to be both tight on time and on money, for instance. Nor is the list exhaustive – I'm sure you can think of other situations when you've run up an emotional overdraft. My aim here is to show you that these are the most common times when it happens – the danger points. And that, if you find yourself repeatedly dipping into your emotional reserves when you're in these circumstances, you're not alone.

The 10 drivers of an emotional overdraft

Recognizing the situations is useful but it only gets us so far. If human beings were rational and sensible all the time, we would always make decisions that benefit our businesses without damaging our personal wellbeing, no matter what the circumstance. Clearly, as the research shows, this doesn't happen.

My second question, therefore, was: *'Why did you choose to draw on your emotional reserves rather than find a different solution?'* This was designed to elicit the underlying reasons for each person's behaviour in a variety of situations – the source of their decision making. If I could understand that, I'd be a lot closer to being able to help people make changes that would have a positive impact on them. The answers I received led me to create what I call the 10 drivers of an emotional overdraft. I've listed them here, together with examples of the comments my respondents gave.

1. **Trust:** I only trust myself; I don't trust others; I want to retain control.
2. **Urgency:** I'm short of time; I'm acting on reflex; I'm not thinking.
3. **Expectation:** it's normal to feel stressed; it's my habit.
4. **Duty:** it's my job; there's no alternative; the buck stops with me.
5. **JFDI (Just Flipping Do It):** I get stuff done; I'm a doer.
6. **Cost:** we're short of money; we don't have the resources; I can't justify the expense.
7. **At a loss:** I'm out of ideas; I've no other solution.

8. **Load-balancing:** I have a short-term need; I'm stepping in to fill a gap.
9. **Empathy:** I'm part of the team; I'm showing care and commitment; I feel guilty if I don't.
10. **Self-worth:** it makes me feel needed; my work is important to me.

Did you find a wry smile creeping across your face as you read this list? Were you nodding along? If so, it's because these drivers are so common. One of my clients, Anne, a leader in an outsourced HR services company, certainly recognized my findings. It happened to be in the run-up to Christmas when we had our regular meeting, and she was under pressure. A team member had resigned, leaving her short-staffed, and on top of that there had been a death in her extended family. Because having a warm culture was important to her business, she'd created an annual tradition of giving a 'let's celebrate our personal successes' presentation to her staff before they broke for the festive season. While she recognized that this was a great way to send everyone off with a warm glow, leading to less likelihood of them deciding to look for a new job in the new year, she was now regretting making this rod for her own back.

On top of everything, there were the staff presents to wrap. She couldn't ask anyone else to do that for her as they were all flat out delivering on deadlines for an important client. So, Anne spent some of her regular Wednesday off – the day she always promised to keep sacrosanct for herself – wrapping the presents. She told herself that it was 'just this once' and that with Christmas, a high client workload, fewer staff and family issues to contend with, it was an exceptional situation. However, if she was honest with herself, she resented it. As she said to me, 'It's not really work, but if you spend your day off wrapping presents and writing nice cards, it's not really a day off either.' The drivers of Anne's drawing on her emotional overdraft were load-balancing (dipping into her personal time to get the business ready for Christmas) and empathy (wanting to show that she was 'with' her team by giving them gifts with a personal touch). We could even throw in a dose of 'JFDI' and 'At a loss' as well.

You might be wondering what other option Anne had to spending her day off wrapping staff gifts. Surely, given the circumstances, there wasn't anything else she could have done? And yet, aren't there always urgent tasks to deal with? Do you ever have enough resources to handle them all? And if you always leap to doing things yourself rather than working out a better solution, won't you be forever drawing on your emotional overdraft? In the next section of the book, we'll be exploring each of the 10 drivers of emotionally costly behaviour. You'll discover alternative ways of handling difficult situations, which – out of habit – you haven't made time to explore, because dipping into your emotional overdraft is less taxing in the short term.

Emotional complexity

In the interests of clarity, I've presented the 10 drivers as if they're pretty straightforward, but you don't have to be an expert in human psychology to know that things aren't always as simple as that. For a start, it's possible to feel different emotions at the same time. Imagine that your best friend is up for the same business award as you, and you're the one who wins it. You feel delighted that you get to hold the trophy but at the same time conflicted, because you feel badly for your friend who was unsuccessful.

It's also become clear to me through my research that an emotional overdraft is linked not only to our work but also to our personal lives. In Anne's case, the death in her family put an emotional strain on her, which made her less resilient when it came to dealing with urgent business issues; possibly, that was part of the reason she decided to wrap the presents herself rather than seek a different solution. And in the opposite direction, using her day off as overflow for work tasks had a compound effect when it came to giving herself space to deal with the pressure she was under.

What's more, our emotions are prone to rising and falling in a volatile manner; sometimes they don't even hang around long enough for us to see that they're there, let alone know what they are. It's not easy to separate them out and give them a neat label, so be kind to yourself if you find yourself struggling with this. It will become easier when you're more practised at identifying the most important drivers for you.

An emotional overdraft is not inevitable

It would be easy to look at the eight situations and the 10 drivers and say, 'Well, that's just what running a business is like. If you can't deal with it, go and get an easier job.' I understand that point of view because it's what most people think. Only the other day, I saw a social media post that listed the 'Five Failings of Leaders'. For a start, I took exception to the word 'failings' because I see them as learnings, not failings. However, it was reading the fifth failing that got me riled up the most: 'If you're not leading from the front, you're failing.' After counting to 10 to calm myself down, I responded that there are countless styles of leadership, not all of which involve leading from the front.

This is just one of many harmful myths about leading a business, with the idea that it has to be emotionally costly being another. When people say to me, 'I'm the type of person who always rolls up my sleeves and gets stuff done', I invite them to see this in another light. Given that we create our experience of the world from inside our own heads, the idea that we're a 'doer' or a 'fixer' is simply a story we've told ourselves. Sometimes, being a 'doer' might be the best solution to a problem, but it certainly isn't in every situation. Often, it turns you into being the person who has the answer to every problem in your business, and then you become a bottleneck. I've worked with many clients who've taught themselves to behave differently to this and it's created brilliant opportunities for the rest of their team to flourish.

Similarly false is the notion that you can't afford to hire staff or bring in more resources to handle a busy workload. I love this saying from entrepreneur Steve Bartlett: 'Anything that costs you your mental health is too expensive.'[17] Whenever

---

[17] See Steve Bartlett's post at: https://linkedin.com/posts/stevenbartlett-123_anything-that-costs-your-mental-health-is-activity-6798872053882662912-hTt4/ [accessed 26 September 2023].

you draw on your emotional overdraft to solve a problem that you think you can't afford to solve by bringing in more help, you're ignoring that hidden line on the P&L which relates to your personal wellbeing. Someone, somewhere, always pays the price.

The prevailing belief that founders and leaders must always be struggling is so strong that it might take a while for you to shift your view. But it's important that you do because, in my research, half of the respondents said that they 'usually' drew on their emotional overdraft, almost half said 'sometimes' and only 3% 'rarely'. When I asked whether they ever 'paid back' their emotional overdraft, an amazing 65% claimed that it was never cleared, and that for almost all of them, this was having an impact on their physical health. Perhaps the saddest thing I learned was that everyone felt this had a negative impact on those around them.

The most gratifying aspect of my research, however, was when I asked people if they would do something about their emotional overdraft if they could. They all (bar one) said yes. And it is possible. I know business leaders who aren't constantly in an emotionally overdrawn state. They sleep well at night and are also brilliantly high achieving, possibly because they've understood Productivity Ninja Graham Allcott's view that when you can't get everything done (which you never can), there are three options available to you:

1. Worry about it and beat yourself up with stress.
2. Identify a 'route through' – work like a horse until you get to the end, keeping sane in the knowledge that you're moving as productively and effectively as you can.

3. Get some help. Hire someone. Call in some favours. Delegate. After all, many hands make light work.[18]

I'm a fan of the second two options but I see the first one far too often. And the good news is that there are alternatives, which is what we'll look at next.

The bottom line

- There are eight types of situations in which you're most likely to run up an emotional overdraft. These are the 'when' of your emotionally costly behaviour.

- There are 10 main drivers of the behaviour that leads you to draw on your emotional reserves. These are the 'why'.

- Situations, emotions and drivers of behaviour sometimes get mixed up with one another, can come and go rapidly, and aren't always easy to recognize.

- It's possible to lead a business without being in a permanently overdrawn state.

---

[18] See: https://productivemuslim.com/achieve-and-maintain-calm/ [accessed 29 July 2023].

5

Monitoring Your Emotional Overdraft

IN THE NEXT part of the book, we'll explore each of the 10 drivers of emotionally costly behaviour and what you can do about them. By the end, you'll have a multitude of ideas for how you can make work and life easier and more enjoyable for yourself. Before we dive into that, however, I'm asking you to start tracking and measuring your overdraft. This has three key benefits:

- It makes the overdraft seem less worrying and daunting because you can see what's happening. It's not an invisible flux of worry and stress, but something that you can place in front of you and analyze.

- You'll notice patterns emerging, which will give you useful feedback. For instance, you might see that you're repeatedly avoiding delegating tasks because you don't trust your team to do things properly. Often, simply being aware of where you're going off track is enough to course-correct you.

- You can make it a critical measure in your management information, thereby allowing the invisible line in the P&L to become more tangible. In future, this could be the catalyst for major organizational behaviour change and also hold the key to unlocking the potential of your business.

Your monitoring will build on the self-knowledge that you gained from the self-assessment quiz you took earlier, which gave you an overview of the size and nature of your emotional overdraft. Now you're being more specific so that you have some areas to focus on. In my experience, when people go through this process they gain immediate insights even before they get to the end of it; self-awareness is a powerful tool.

The number method

You're going to record the changes in your emotional overdraft each day for 28 days. There are two methods that you can use. Most people I work with prefer to use what I call the number method, but there's another that I'll cover in a moment which might appeal to you as well (see Figure 2). For the number method, this is what you do:

- Choose a way of recording things that works for you. It could be a spreadsheet, a notebook, a Word document or anything that allows you to set down information. Alternatively, download a template to fill in at www.emotionaloverdraft.com

- Award yourself a starting score of 100; this will set a benchmark point for your emotional overdraft.

- At the end of every day before you go to bed, give yourself a score. If you think your emotional overdraft has increased that day, score the day as +1 (your emotional overdraft has risen); if it's decreased, score the day as –1 (your emotional overdraft has decreased); and if it's stayed the same, score the day as 0.

- Jot a short note beside each day's score with the reasons why you gave it. What happened that day which had an impact on your resilience?

- At the end of your first week, tally up your score and add the result to the benchmark. So, if you had four days when your emotional overdraft increased, two when it decreased, and one when it stayed the same (a net change of +2), your score moves from 100 to 102. This means that, over the whole week, your emotional overdraft has increased.

- Review your week's score and your notes and ask yourself whether any patterns are emerging. Is there anything that surprises you? What have you learned so far? Record these reflections.

Repeat your review at the end of each week. At the end of the 28 days you can stop, but if you've found the process helpful feel free to carry on for another month. You can also consider including your emotional overdraft monitoring in your company's management information on an ongoing basis (see Chapter 18 for more on this).

	Date	Direction (use -1, 0, 1) -1 emotional overdraft reduced 0 - emotional overdraft unchanged 1 emotional overdraft extended		emotional /overdraft
Day 1				
Day 2	1-May			Notes
Day 3	2-May			
Day 4	3-May	-1		
Day 5	4-May	1		Great day, big project completed
Day 6	5-May	0		IT issues all day, barely got through any of to do list, had to work late
Day 7	6-May	1		Doing the job
Day 8	7-May	-1		Issues with the team, client
Day 9	8-May	-1		Great team building session / happy client
Day 10	9-May	-1		Sunshine / Day off

Figure 2   An example of the number method

Try to resist the temptation to complicate the methodology. You could, for instance, take away three points for an absolutely terrible day rather than one point, but I'm not sure that would bring you more clarity. Also, it's important that you record your scores and comments daily because, after two or three days have gone by, you'll forget the details; you'll be influenced by what happened most recently instead of pinpointing how it felt at the time. And please don't skip the weekends. Your emotional overdraft is just as active then as it is during the working week, and many of my clients who've done this have been surprised at how much their work was affecting their home life and vice versa. It's important that you recognize this, whether it be positive or negative.

Interpreting your results

At the end of the month, what do you observe? Has your emotional overdraft increased or decreased since the beginning? And what were the main drivers of the change? You now have a body of reference which will give you a concrete sense of how your emotional overdraft fluctuated throughout that month, and an indication of whether your decision making has been at the cost of your own resilience.

Please bear in mind that these are soft metrics using notional numbers. One hundred is an arbitrary figure and is there simply to give you a starting point so you can see whether your overdraft is going up or down. For that reason, your score isn't one that you can compare with anybody else's, nor is it a good idea to try. We all have different levels of resilience, and these will vary from time to time. For instance, some of us are like long-distance runners who can keep going all day as long as we don't exert ourselves too much, whereas others are like sprinters who need a burst of energy to power through a task. There's no right or wrong in that. All you're trying to achieve here is some deeper understanding about yourself and how you experience your emotional overdraft.

Stephen was one of my clients who gained valuable insights from this process. Nine years ago, he co-founded a branding consultancy with his wife Katrina. When he carried out the tracking and measurement, he noticed that the days when his emotional overdraft grew larger were those when he stepped in to do something that would ideally have been done by one of his team, or should have been handled by a standard operating procedure. For instance, when a request for a unique piece of work came, or a task that only he or Katrina could handle because it involved a high-stakes financial investment, such as purchasing a new office building. He called these situations 'grit in the cogs'

– the things that stopped the well-oiled machine of the company from functioning without his input. Conversely, neutral days were those when the business was running smoothly and he could do his job without worrying about other people's work.

He also found it helpful to monitor his emotions at the weekends because it taught him that recharging then was far more than a neutral activity; it was essential for increasing his resilience. This was in contrast to when he and Katrina first set up the business and had to work at weekends and bank holidays just to keep up (the 'founders' curse', as he put it). He also noticed what he called the 'multiplier effect' when running a business with his spouse. For every hour that he and Katrina spent talking about work when they were at home, it felt like double the points because of the negative impact on his recuperation time. On the other hand, when they had a big win at work, being able to celebrate it with her led to double the benefit.

The building block method

As we've previously identified, emotions are complex and go up and down during the day. This means that when you're completing your audit at the end of each day, you might find yourself wondering what score to give. Suppose you started the morning by finding out that you'd won a piece of new business, and you also promoted a member of staff who really deserved it. Then, you received an email from someone you employed 10 years ago who's now become the MD of a company, and who wanted to thank you for teaching him so much.

This sent your resilience levels sky high. But after lunch, your biggest client called to say that they weren't going to work with you anymore. No sooner had you put the phone down on that piece of crushing news than your son's school phoned to announce that you had to pick him up because he had chickenpox. What do you write down for that day? Did your emotional overdraft get larger or smaller? Or did the highs and lows cancel themselves out so that it was neutral?

This is a good question. One answer is simply to give the score that you feel best reflects the overall day, but the other is to use what I call the building block method. I created this a long time ago to help me understand my emotions and resilience levels as they fluctuated throughout the day. At the time, I was wanting to see if there were particular periods when I was not as effective as I could be, but it works equally well for monitoring your emotional overdraft.

The building block method involves you having some fun by buying a bunch of Lego blocks in different colours and a board to stick them on (Figure 3). It works like this:

- Every half hour during the day, put a block on your board. If you feel that you've drawn on your emotional overdraft in that time, choose a red block. If you feel more resilient than you did half an hour before, choose green. And if it's neither one nor the other, choose yellow.

- At the end of the day, review your tower of blocks and see how things went up and down for you. Can you see a prevalence of a certain colour of block?

Figure 3   An example of the building block method

The reason this is helpful is that it gives you a way of seeing your day that reflects how it was at the time, rather than only reviewing it at the end and having to remember. You might also start to see patterns emerge of energy and resilience levels fluctuating throughout the day, which will give you useful information. It's a visual and tactile process that will appeal to you if you're that way inclined. Alternatively, if the colour aspect is something you'd find useful, but not the building blocks, I've known people to use coloured pens on paper, cells in a spreadsheet, and sticky notes. Play with what works for you. It's not a method I recommend using on an ongoing basis because it can become one more thing to do in your day, but you can use it when you want more insight. I dip back into it every now and then when I think it will be helpful.

A good example of how this method can work well is with a current client of mine, Sabrina. She has to pick up her daughter from school at 3:45 pm each day – an obviously immovable deadline. This can create a huge amount of stress because even if her clients are shouting and the world is falling around her ears, she has to down tools and leave. What's more, there's a nasty sting in the tail: she feels guilty that she resents having to interrupt her day, and yet she wants to do it and knows it's important for her relationship with her daughter (the emotional overdraft can be spiteful like that). Using the building blocks has helped her to recognize when the peaks and troughs of stress are happening; she can't change her commitment to her daughter, but she can be more aware of the impact it's having on her resilience.

The bottom line

- Monitoring your emotional overdraft helps you to analyze what's going on in your day; this in itself can be helpful for reducing stress levels.

- It also gives you insights into the situations that drain your overdraft; often, simply knowing this can help you to change your behaviour.

- The number method involves giving yourself a daily score and analyzing it at the end of each week and at the end of the month.

- The building block method gives you a way of tracking your overdraft over the course of each day.

- Whatever method you use, monitoring your emotional overdraft can end up being a critical piece of management information that has the potential to transform how you lead your business.

Part Three
How to Reduce
Your Emotional
Overdraft

6

The 10 Drivers of an Emotional Overdraft

THE NEXT 10 chapters explore the drivers of the behaviours that increase your emotional overdraft and hold your business back. They increase your emotional overdraft because they overload your thinking about the way you work, and they hold your business back because they impact your performance as a leader. Here's why these two factors are important.

Overloading your thinking. The drivers we'll be exploring don't represent bad things that you have to change. In fact, these drivers are simply ways of thinking and behaving that can either support you or diminish you, and my aim is to show you how to make them work for you rather than against you. Given that your thinking creates your feelings, which create your behaviour, which drives the

7
Trust

'I only trust myself'
'I don't trust others'
'I want to retain control'

THE FIRST DRIVER of the emotional overdraft is not trusting other people to get on with their jobs. I'm sure I don't need to tell you what this does to your wellbeing because you're probably only too familiar with it: constantly worrying about whether work is being done to your standards, juggling too many balls, working late every night and doing the wrong things – tasks that are other people's responsibility but that you can't seem to stop yourself from taking on. This can be exhausting, demoralizing and a drain on your resilience.

From my work with many leaders, I find that they're usually aware they have a trust issue but they still find it hard to change. Trust is emotional because it centres on our most fundamental human need – for safety. When we entrust someone with something that matters greatly to us, it can make us feel vulnerable; we don't give away our trust lightly because we're afraid of what will happen if it turns out to be misplaced. Take what happened when everybody started working from home during the Covid-19 pandemic, for example. Many leaders and managers were alarmed at the prospect of their staff not being visible at their desks, and worried that they'd spend their days watching TV and lounging around in their pyjamas. How could they control people if they weren't in the office? But in fact, the opposite happened. Without the physical separation between work and home, many of those same staff ended up working too hard and found it difficult to switch off, with a fair degree of burnout being the result.

What happens when you don't trust people

Trusting people is fundamental to growing your business, because if you don't:

- They become demotivated

- Your company stagnates

- Your emotional overdraft grows ever larger

That sounds unsustainable to me, so let's unpack the downsides and explore them.

Your staff become demotivated

I had a client, Zara, who'd been internally promoted to MD of her company, and who spent many months fretting about whether she should sack a senior member of her team. The person was uncooperative, difficult to get on with and not even very good at his job. However, she felt that he was also popular with other members of the team and was very much a political player, gaining the ear of everybody around him to bring them over to his side. She was worried that, if she let him go, the reaction of others would be negative and damage the business. In the end, after many sleepless nights, she released him as kindly as she could and called her team together to explain the situation. She was expecting disbelief and objections, but to her surprise they said that they were amazed he'd lasted so long. It turned out that they'd long felt uncomfortable with his political back-channelling but hadn't felt able to do anything about it. What a relief for her, but also what a demotivating experience for her staff to have gone through all those months. If only she'd trusted them to see through his behaviour, she could have saved a lot of heartache all round.

Often, lack of trust can be caused by assuming that people can't perform tasks competently without you. But let's think about what might happen if you *did* trust them. As long as they have the right level of support and training, and you're asking them to carry out work that's within (or just outside) their capabilities, there's no reason why they shouldn't work well without micromanagement. They'll have the opportunity to rise to challenges and deal with unexpected and difficult situations, allowing them to grow and develop. And they'll enjoy their work more because they feel respected, leading them to want to take on more responsibility. This is borne out by research. Compared with people at low-trust companies, people at high-trust companies report 74% less stress, 50% higher productivity, 13% fewer sick days, 76% more engagement, 29% more satisfaction with their lives and 40% less burnout.[20] It's a virtuous circle.

If, on the other hand, you don't trust people to get on with things, they'll feel demotivated. Their day-to-day work will be unchallenging and monotonous; they won't be learning anything new; they'll feel bored and resentful about their skills not being respected; and they'll start to wonder if they should look for another job. Or, rather, the good people will; the mediocre ones will hunker down and carry on doing their humdrum work. It's a vicious circle.

Your company stagnates

Cast your mind back to when you first started your business. It's possible that you were the main expert in the services it was providing, and you might also have been the administrator, the finance manager, the HR person and the marketing head. Then, as the company grew, you started to recruit people to fill some of those roles, and you had to trust them to do their jobs. Now you've moved from two people to five, to 10, to 20, your expert skills have become less current and you've become more of a

---

[20] See: www.linkedin.com/feed/update/urn:li:activity:70306036 84916977664/ [accessed 29 July 2023].

manager and less of a 'doer'. Nor do you know all your staff intimately like you did in the early days, which makes it harder to trust them.

That's the challenge of growth, and it's not easy. But the longer it takes for you to trust people, the more it will stop your business flourishing. Lack of trust has an impact on your culture, manifesting itself in time-consuming micromanagement, draconian rules that cater for the lowest common denominator, and staff being unwilling to take risks and push themselves beyond their well-worn boundaries. When employees don't have the autonomy to take the initiative and innovate, that's when the rot sets in.

I once worked with a client, Carlos, who was an excellent graphic designer and had been running his own design agency for 20 years. During that time, the technology he'd used when he first started slowly become ancient history, so when he wandered around the studio to see what his designers were working on, he found it hard to assess how well they were doing. This led him to insist that they did things the 'old' way, even though he knew that didn't make sense. I helped him to realize that he needed to recruit a studio manager who would run the studio for him. Carlos was nervous about investing in a new hire and didn't have the budget to bring in someone as experienced as he'd have liked; however, he did find a person who had the right skills. When he realized that the new manager was transforming how effectively the designers worked, it was a watershed moment. He stopped stifling everyone's talent and started to trust people, eventually becoming the leader of a successful company that went from strength to strength. But it could so easily have gone the other way.

Your emotional overdraft grows ever larger

You should be building an enterprise in which you're the *least* capable person in the room. You need to employ people who have specialist expertise and perform their roles better than you ever could. As founder or leader, you're always going to be the most important person, but if you want a company that's scalable you must be willing to accept that there will come a point at which you've brought in so many brilliant people that you're almost not needed anymore.

While the idea of being 'redundant' in your business might seem scary, you can think of it as a liberation. When the company stops being dependent on you, it gives you the glorious opportunity to focus on doing what you love. It might be that recruiting and training people is what lights you up, or maybe you relish rolling up your sleeves and delving into the technical stuff, just like you did before you hired staff. How exciting would it be to wake up in the morning knowing that all you had to do was what you enjoyed, because you trusted people to handle everything else? What would that do for your emotional overdraft?

How to build your ability to trust

I'm making being trusting sound like it should be easy but, as you know from experience, it rarely is. Because our reluctance to trust people comes from our hardwired need for safety, it's something that you need to make a conscious decision to change. The key to this is realizing that, while feeling able to trust someone might seem as if it's all about them and their performance capabilities, it's mostly about you. Here are some straightforward, practical actions you can choose to take in order to make it easier to trust your teams:

- Recruit well

- Train well

- Structure well

- Plan well

- Delegate well

- Monitor well

- Get over yourself

Recruit well

If you don't trust your staff to do a good job, the first thing to look at is the way you recruited them. What do you look for in a new hire? What's most important to you? To me, attitude is the most fundamental quality in an employee, way ahead of skills and experience. You can always train people in skills, and they'll naturally gain experience, but you can't teach attitude. Make sure that you hire people with 'batteries included'; if, when you interview them, you sense that there's energy and commitment lacking, don't give them a job no matter how skilled they are. Ask yourself if you'd feel comfortable entrusting them with an important and challenging task – would they be up for it?

Train well

When I talk to leaders about trusting their staff, the conversation often goes like this: 'I know I don't delegate enough and I need to trust my team more, so I'm going to give Asim a task. It's part of his job and it's something he should be able to manage, so let's see what happens. If Asim does well, I'll give him more responsibility next time. But if he messes up, it proves I shouldn't have trusted him in the first place.' So off they go and delegate the task to Asim, but without enough guidance or support. Unsurprisingly, Asim does a bad job of it. It's as if the leader has unconsciously sabotaged their opportunity to trust him because they would rather be proved right than get better at delegating.

Assuming that Asim was hired correctly, this tells me not that he has a problematic attitude, but that he hasn't been adequately trained. The process of training starts when you plan out a new role and decide what skills are needed for it. If the person you've hired for the role doesn't have those skills, you need to teach them.

Training is one of those things that always feels as if it can wait. Many companies I work with tell me that they allocate a certain percentage of their staff's time to learning, but that it rarely happens because they're too busy. Then, surprise surprise, the end of the year rolls around and those people are not performing as well as they could be because they haven't learnt new skills. Some leaders even have a belief that people learn by 'osmosis', just by being around each other in the office. That's not true. What it actually means is that there's no proper training for those people, and no systematic identification of the skills gaps that need to be filled. When you have a team of well-trained staff, it's a lot easier to trust them to do their jobs to a high standard.

Structure well

People need to understand what their responsibilities are if they're to do a trustworthy job. As with training, this begins with a role description (not a job description – that's too task oriented). Some leaders find the idea of role descriptions constricting, or maybe they've just never got around to creating them, but it's not fair on your staff for them not to know where the boundaries of their roles lie. In my experience, when people are clear on what their roles are, *and* have the relevant levels of autonomy and authority to carry them out, they're more than capable of being proactive and doing their jobs to a high standard.

Plan well

It's important to have a plan for your business that you communicate to all your employees. If they understand the broad arc of your journey – the pole star you're trying to follow – they'll line up behind you. But when people don't know what they're aiming at, they'll pull in different directions and it's hard for them to know what to do. This can manifest itself in them not doing what they're told, misunderstanding your instructions and coming across as obstructive and unhelpful.

Communicating your overall objective is also important when it comes to the little things. An example of this was when I was arranging an off-site meeting for a group of employees that would involve us all staying overnight in a hotel the night before. I thought it would be a nice idea to book a restaurant for dinner that evening, but when I asked one of the women who was attending what time she would arrive, all she could talk about was the uncertainties of the traffic. I found myself feeling increasingly irritated, wondering if she even wanted to come to the meal, and then realized that I'd not told her about the dinner; all I'd done was to ask her when she thought she'd get there. Once I'd explained myself, she said, 'Oh, I can leave at 4:00 to beat the traffic. See you then.'

Delegate well

A client of mine, Joshua, was frustrated. He'd asked a member of his team to do something that he believed was relatively simple, yet important: 'a 10-minute task at most'. When the task remained incomplete by the date my client needed it by, he was annoyed and instantly recalled other times when the person had failed in a similar way. His conclusion? That he couldn't trust them, and that his people weren't capable of delivering without being micromanaged. Given that we know trusting people is more about us than it is about them, it's important to look inward before kicking out. So, we explored this and here's what it turns out that Joshua had actually said to his employee: 'Please can you change that piece of copy on the website? It's a 10-minute job.' What he could have said was: 'We're planning a new marketing campaign that will drive people to the site. They'll look at the product page but there's an error on it. We go live on Thursday, so could you tweak the error by Wednesday evening please. It's a small but important job. Could you drop me a line to let me know when it's been done?'

What's the difference? The second approach has a context, a deadline and a specific action request. With his original request, how could the person have known when the change needed to be done by? Describing it as 'a 10-minute job' made it seem as if it wasn't critical. What's more, in my opinion few jobs are 'just 10-minute jobs'; usually, those who believe they are have never undertaken that task themselves. Clarity in delegation is essential if you want to trust people to do what you want.

It's also important to understand that you may have a different working style to the person you're delegating to. Suppose you're a detail person. If you ask someone who's of a similar mindset to write a report, they'll probably come back to you with the level of information you're after. Great, you think – I can definitely trust them. But if they happen to be a big picture person, they may give you a report that's conceptual and top-level. They assume that they've done what you wanted, but you feel annoyed. This is where transparency comes in. If you explain your preferences and help the person to understand exactly what you want, they're more likely to earn your trust.

Monitor well

One of the main things that might stop you from trusting your employees is not knowing whether they're doing a good job of something. It may be a task that matters a lot to you or one that – as an expert yourself – you believe you could do better than them. On the other hand, maybe you don't know enough about it to be confident that you can assess their performance. Somehow, trusting them when they say 'It's all going fine' doesn't really cut it for you. So, what do you do? If you've recruited and trained them well, and if they have clear role descriptions, you're part way towards being able to trust them already. But there's a further element, which is monitoring how they're getting on.

Do you continuously appraise your staff performance? Not just once a year (what use is that, really?) but as you go along? When people know if they're mastering, delivering and developing their capabilities, they understand whether they're doing well enough and so do you. Employees are entitled to go home each day with a clear knowledge of whether they've performed at the level expected of them; if they're not sure, they'll end up not trusting you and you won't trust them.

Part of appraisal is putting in place a measurement system for your staff's development. Some leaders call them goals, some key performance indicators (KPIs), some objectives and key results (OKRs) – it doesn't matter what label they have, they're simply a way of allowing people to be specific about whether they've achieved or not achieved. They bring clarity to both you and them. And, like with appraisals, they need to be monitored way more often than once a year because with support at the right time, and with some training or additional resources, a person who's failing at something might well succeed.

You should also set 'gates', or milestones, for delegated projects or tasks, and ask the people you've asked to carry them out to report back to you. This helps you to relax because you're not worrying about whether they're doing okay; they'll be checking in with you at specific times. Imagine what it would do for your emotional overdraft if you were to give someone a clear brief, with enough context and detail for them to know how you want it carried out, and to be confident that they'll tell you on pre-agreed dates how they're progressing.

Get over yourself

I appreciate that this sounds a bit harsh, but I mean it in a tongue-in-cheek way. All the practical steps I've given you here will help you to create a framework for a more trusting relationship with your teams, but, sometimes, despite changes in procedures and working practices, you might still find yourself struggling to trust them. It's such a hard habit to break, and I understand why. Your business is your baby, and just as a parent finds themselves wiping away a tear when they drop their precious child off at school on the first day, so a founder finds it a wrench to hand important tasks and projects to others.

This is when it helps to remember that lack of trust is an emotional issue, and therefore might need an emotional solution. It could be therapy, talking things over with a friend or colleague, or maybe just giving yourself a bit of a talking to. Whatever you need, please do it, because lack of trust is one of the most common and corrosive ways that leaders build up emotional overdrafts. Your own health, and that of your business, depend on it.

The bottom line

- Not trusting people to carry out tasks properly is a key driver of an emotional overdraft, leading to working long hours and excessive stress.

- It also demotivates your staff and stifles your business growth, as you will always be the bottleneck in your company.

- There are numerous practical measures you can put in place that make it easier to trust people, such as creating new recruitment, training and planning processes.

- You can also do this by delegating with clarity, monitoring progress and – if necessary – seeking the emotional support you need to change.

8
Urgency

'I'm short of time'
'I'm acting on reflex'
'I'm not thinking'

WE'VE ALL BEEN in a situation like this. It's mid-morning on a Thursday and you've just come out of a finance meeting. Your head of operations grabs you on your way back to your desk and tells you that one of your clients is demanding a complex piece of work a week earlier than agreed. Before you've had a chance to digest this news, your phone rings. It's your IT manager, whose car has just been broken into. He has to get it fixed, so the system upgrade that was planned for this afternoon will have to wait until tomorrow. If you can't find someone else to handle it, some of your client deliverables will be delayed; the problem is, he's your only safe pair of hands. Now you have to contact those clients and reassure them before they start wondering what's going on, and that's before you've even dealt with the other urgent request. Your day, which looked reasonably organized when you first arrived, is starting to resemble a disaster zone.

Staggering from one crisis to another is a key driver for an emotional overdraft. You feel as if you never do anything properly and are always acting on reflex; instead of working out how to solve problems in a constructive way, you're only worrying about how you can extinguish the fire in front of you before it ignites the entire office. That also means you're shunting other tasks onto the back burner, which makes you feel even more stressed.

What happens when you act out of urgency

Let's be honest. Being in urgent mode doesn't always feel bad – it can be a buzz to be at the centre of the storm. There's nothing like throwing yourself into a crisis to make you feel important and needed, like a superhero saving the day. Some people are even addicted to it.

That's fine when it's only the occasional emergency, but what happens when it happens a lot? For a start, it's stressful. Humans were never designed to operate on adrenaline for substantial parts of the week, which is why being under pressure can be a key factor in many health problems. Also, you don't make the best decisions when you're in that state of mind. Instead of thinking through a situation calmly and clearly, you leap to the most obvious solution – the one that you can implement the quickest and that will give you the most superficially beneficial result. It's the fast food of decision making.

And what about the impact on the people around you? If you're dealing with urgent problems yourself, it can make your colleagues feel unappreciated and helpless. Some of them may be thinking, 'Here we go again. If only we'd planned this properly, we wouldn't have the boss panicking as usual. Why is it always like this? Why do I stay here? It's a nightmare.' Then there's the effect on your family and friends when you get back home. People who are on a come-down from an adrenaline high aren't easy to be around; their energy is spent and they sometimes have little interest in the problems of others. Being the partner of someone who's been acting out of urgency for much of the day can be a lonely experience.

Mira, a client of mine, was one person who had this issue. As the founder and MD of an academic tutoring business, she regularly worked long hours, especially during the run-up to exam time in the summer. This was having a negative impact on her relationship with her husband. When she got busy, she would ask him if he would do her share of the cooking and housework, which he agreed to, but for him this was at the expense of other things that were important to him. At the end of that period, they would always feel burned out, and she'd still be coping with the aftermath two months later. No matter how much she prepared herself for the busy season, it never seemed to get any easier. What could she do?

How to stop acting out of urgency

Of course, some things are always going to be urgent. It's impossible to run a business without the odd curve ball hitting you; people will go off sick, clients will have last-minute demands and there's always the potential for something that's outside of your control to go wrong. And yet, there are other ways to approach urgent situations than the ones which end up becoming a driver for your emotional overdraft. Some of them relate to how you see the urgent situation in the moment and others are more about how you set up your business to avoid emergencies in the first place. Some suggestions are to:

- See urgency for what it really is

- Use urgency as a springboard for change

- Plan ahead

- Bombproof your business with processes

- Revisit your commercials

See urgency for what it really is

Unlike trust, which is an internal driver, urgency is an external one. Something has happened that needs to be dealt with right now – so it's urgent. But is it really? As we explored in Chapter 3, it's not events outside of us that create our emotions but the quality of our thinking about them. A last-minute demand might seem urgent, but we can only deliver what's possible in the time available; the urgency comes from our thoughts about it rather than the thing itself. I noticed this phenomenon in action when

I first started out in the advertising industry many years ago. The head of production in the agency I was in was a grizzled old warrior who'd seen hundreds of urgent campaigns come and go over the years, and whenever I came to him with a rush print job that needed to be completed 'now', his response was: 'There's always time to reprint, my son, there's always time to reprint.' In other words, when the inevitable errors occurred on a piece of marketing material that had been fast-tracked through, strangely enough, there was always enough space in the schedule to start the job again from scratch and still deliver on time.

When you start to see urgency as something that you've created in your own mind, interesting solutions are more likely to present themselves. Mira, who I mentioned before, began questioning what urgency meant to her. What was leading to it? What decisions had she made prior to the urgent situation that meant it arose in the first place? Was it really an emergency or was it self-created? Could she allow other people to save the day? And maybe – just maybe – did the day need to be saved in the first place?

When you question the reality of urgency, you can sometimes find that what seemed urgent isn't in fact so. I remember a day when one of my team was all set to cancel a long weekend away that she'd been looking forward to for months. It was because a client had told her that he desperately needed something for Monday, and she felt she had no alternative but to work. I said to her, 'Have you told the client that you're going on holiday? Does he really need it for Monday or could he wait until Tuesday?' She called the client and it turned out that he was fine to wait another day – the last thing he wanted was to ruin her trip. It's always worth checking whether something is as urgent as you think.

Use urgency as a springboard for change

Another way to stop urgency becoming a driver for your emotional overdraft is to re-frame it as an opportunity to think afresh. The nature of acting on reflex is that we don't think critically about what we're doing – we dive in and bash a problem on the head rather than working out if there's a better way to solve it. You can ask your team what caused the emergency and whether there's anything you could put in place to stop it happening again; maybe an improvement in processes or planning procedures is in order. Another idea is to use it as a catalyst for innovation. If the situation is the result of a client last-minute request, for instance, is there a product you can develop that would cater for this eventuality for others as well? Could it become part of your standard offering?

The beauty of seeing urgency as a springboard for something new is that not only are you likely to come up with fresh ways of working, but you can also counter the stress-related increase in your emotional overdraft with the excitement of change. Something positive has come out of what would otherwise have been a wholly negative situation and that makes you feel better in its own right.

Plan ahead

Sometimes, a task is urgent because it's genuinely unexpected. But, more often than not, it's because we haven't planned things properly – or if we have, we haven't stuck to the plan. The more organized we are in the first place, the easier it is to deal with the genuinely unexpected events that inevitably come our way. Being organized, however, seems tough when we're crazy busy. Who has time for that? And so it goes on.

This is where you need to take a long, hard look at how you plan the work in your business. Many people say that they could never have foreseen an emergency situation, but, if they're honest with themselves, they probably didn't want to think about it. Urgent is not normally unexpected; in fact, in any business it's most definitely predictable. The question is, why has it become urgent? If you can predict what's coming up (and mostly you can), you can put in place processes and staffing levels to deal with them. The more efficient and organized your business is, the more the urgent things will fall away.

Bombproof your business with processes

A key part of becoming organized is to put in place sound processes. Some people think that following processes limits their creativity, but I don't buy that; having worked in the advertising industry for many years, which is one that thrives on creativity, I've seen how when people do the repeatable work well, the creative work has the space to flourish.

However, while it's simple to spot the need for processes, it's hard to get into the habit of defining them and then making sure that everyone has the training to use them. You also have to adhere to them yourself. I mentioned earlier how hard I used to draw on my emotional overdraft every time I led an advertising pitch. That's because we had a process but we didn't follow it. We appointed a pitch manager who was tasked with organizing it all but we gave the role to a junior member of staff who had no authority to hold anyone to account, so people didn't turn up to the planning meetings. Then, on the day before the pitch, we were always panicking – I've lost count of how many presentations I've rewritten in cafés across the road from the client's offices on the morning itself. Madness.

It's not only routine work that processes are helpful for, but also any kind of potential emergency. For instance, if you run a business that designs and sets up exhibition spaces, there's an immovable deadline for the exhibition itself. But you know that last-minute problems will emerge; an exhibitor will turn up without the right electrical cables, or road works will delay the arrival of delivery vans. What processes have you set up to deal with these predictable problems? If you have a procedure to fall back on, your stress levels will be far lower than if you have to reinvent the wheel each time. One of my clients, who runs a web development agency that has excellent processes, has something that he calls a 'bat phone'. If a website develops problems after launch due to an unknown integration with another site, the bat phone is 'activated'. This mobilizes the people who know how to fix the issue, and because it has a name everyone knows that it's urgent. How much more useful is that than if the company kidded itself nothing was ever going to go wrong?

Revisit your commercials

You're at your desk when your biggest client calls. 'There's good news and bad news,' he says. 'The good news is that I've just had some budget released and I'd like you to spend it on a new project. The bad news is that it needs to happen this week.' What do you do? You don't want to say no to your most important client, but nor do your teams have the capacity to drop everything and pile on to this task. You could swoop in and do it all yourself, which in some circumstances might be the right answer, but how about thinking more commercially about this request?

Should you be paying the price for your client's lack of planning? If you do, you're going to be drawing hard on your emotional overdraft. But what if you use some of that budget to hire freelance staff or find another way to buy yourself out of the stress? Even better, what if you'd anticipated this kind of thing when you first started working with them and included rush fees in your agreement, explaining why they're there? When you have some extra cash to play with, urgent jobs don't feel as stressful because you have options that will ease the pressure on your resilience.

The bottom line

- Deprioritizing important work in favour of urgent work can give you a short-term buzz, but if it happens too often it can lead to burnout and a reduction in business performance.

- It can also damage staff morale, be the cause of poor decision making and have a negative impact on your personal relationships.

- You can reduce the stress involved by understanding that the urgency is created in the mind, and also by using it as a springboard for positive change.

- You can also reduce the number of emergencies you have to deal with by planning ahead, creating processes and charging more for urgent work.

9
Expectation

'It's normal to feel stressed'
'It's my habit'

'WHEN YOU SET up a business, you're in an emotional overdraft right from the start because you have to give up so much to do it. To be a founder is to accept this – it's a necessary part of what you do.'

So said my client Stephen, co-founder of a branding consultancy with his wife Katrina, whom we met in a previous chapter. I give his words as an example because it's what a lot of people assume that running a business is like. There's an expectation that you're often going to be working in a way that makes you feel tired and unhappy, and that the people around you – both colleagues and family – are going to feel the strain as well. Only entrepreneurs who are prepared to power through this stressful, all-consuming experience are worthy of the name.

This is a myth. There are many, many business leaders who don't work in a constant state of stress and low resilience; I know because I work with some of them, and I expect that if you think about it, you do too. They don't dread Mondays, they don't keep themselves going only by dreaming of the day when they can sell up and retire, and if they do have a difficult patch, they make sure that they quickly 'pay off' their emotional overdraft afterwards. To me, this makes sense. If unremitting pressure was an inevitable part of launching and running an organization, how could all of the amazing businesses and innovations that we see around us even exist? Entrepreneurs would be dropping like flies left, right and centre, and while sadly a few do, there are far more who don't.

What happens when you expect to feel stressed

When you expect to feel stressed a lot of the time, you're likely to explain it away as the natural lot of a leader. That means you're not sensitive to the level of stress you're experiencing, which in turn means that you're not inclined to do anything about it. It's a self-fulfilling prophecy.

It can also damage your health. A business-owner friend told me recently that, although he's always loved skiing and playing football, he's done little of them in the past five years because he's been so busy at work. He barely gets out, lunches 'al desko' every day and has stopped going to the gym. Given that he's in his mid-40s, this is the worst possible age for him to stop taking part in sport – he should be looking after his physical fitness so that he can make the most of the rest of his life.

If, on the other hand, you see stress as something that *isn't* inevitable, it encourages you to look for solutions to business problems that don't involve putting pressure on yourself. And if you really can't avoid the short-term pain of an emotional overdraft, you'll look to pay it back as soon as you can so that you can build up your resilience again. Many leaders have an irrational fear that, if they take a lunch break or have a holiday, something terrible will happen. But what would it be? Even if their worst fears were realized, surely it would simply be an opportunity to make their organizations less dependent on them.

How to change your expectations about stress

Everyone feels stress from time to time, and just as some of us have naturally higher or lower levels of resilience than others, so some of us find it relatively easy or hard to cope with pressure. But while it's normal to feel the strain every now and then, it shouldn't be all the time. If expecting to be stressed is habitual for you, changing it will involve you making a conscious effort to see what's going on and deciding to do something about it. It's not a process that will happen naturally. Here are some ways that you can do this:

- Recognize what's going on

- See it as a habit that you can change

- Alter your expectations

- Re-frame your idea of failure

- Seek help from a coach

- Recharge

Recognize what's going on

We live in a culture that tells us it's okay to feel stressed at work – in fact, it's almost expected. How else could we be sure that we're doing a good job? At a company I ran many years ago, if somebody got up from their desk to go home at 5:30 they'd face a chorus of, 'Having a half day, are you?' or 'Popping out for lunch?' When I noticed that this was happening, I raised it as a discussion point at our monthly all-hands meeting and we explored how these comments made us feel. It turned out that some of the people who'd been the most vocal were also those who felt the guiltiest about leaving at a civilized hour, and it seemed that this public shaming had become a toxic behaviour affecting everyone. The second that I called it out, people recognized what was going on and it stopped.

This shows that the first step towards changing your expectations about stress is to hold them up to the light so that they become clear to you. Your emotional overdraft monitoring system comes in useful here, as it's not only an alarm for telling you whether your overdraft is growing larger, it's also a tool for cataloguing the activities that are causing you to have a bad (or a good) day. By giving you an objective view of your experience, it helps you to spot the unconscious habits that you've fallen into, allowing you to look at events using facts rather than emotions.

When you review your notes about the things that lowered your resilience over the course of the month, it's worth reflecting on them and asking yourself what was behind the stress. Just as importantly, think about what caused you to have a good day. What happened that reduced your emotional overdraft, and how can you do more of it in future? As we explored in Chapter 3, we're trained to see the negative rather than the positive, and this causes us to skip past the good things without celebrating them. Don't let these ingrained habits take over your thinking; be more deliberate than that.

Another way of standing back from your feelings and seeing them impartially is by asking yourself, 'What would I expect from other people in these circumstances? Would I want my staff or my family to be in a perpetual state of stress? If one of them told me they were feeling this way, would I tell them that it was what they should expect and to keep hammering away at their work regardless?' I'm sure that wouldn't be your response, and hopefully you have a smile on your face just thinking about how ridiculous it would be. Why shouldn't we be as kind to ourselves as we would be to a friend or colleague?

See it as a habit that you can change

Expecting to feel burdened, stressed and unhappy at work is nothing more than an unhelpful habit, and all habits can be changed. It might take time, but there are some steps you can take to get the ball rolling.

The first is to recognize the habit in the first place. Taking a basic example from my own life, I know that whenever

I make myself a cup of tea, I automatically reach for the cupboard above the kettle where the biscuits are kept; this, I can acknowledge to myself, is a behaviour that I want to change. The next step is to understand the consequences of the habit, which for my biscuit addiction are painfully obvious (okay, a middle-aged spread and a sugar high followed by a low, if you insist on knowing). The third step is to create a better habit in its place. In my case, I could simply stop myself from reaching for the biscuits, but that would involve willpower. So, as I'm trying to get fitter at the gym and need to increase my protein intake, I drink a low-calorie protein shake mid-afternoon to stave off the hunger pangs. It's also important to have goals, which for me is to lose a certain amount of weight. And finally, I can accept that I will sometimes fall off the wagon. My danger zone is when I'm travelling by train and can easily pick up a packet of biscuits without my wife knowing. I'll admit, I've occasionally succumbed to the temptation. But when I have, I've acknowledged to myself that change is hard, and rather than give up and go back to my old ways, I'll just try to be better next time.[21] To summarize:

- Recognize that you're in the habit of living in an emotional overdraft.

- Understand the consequences of it – the lowered resilience, the tiredness, the impact on your relationships.

- Create a better habit in its place, for instance by getting up from your desk and going for a short walk if you

---

[21] See: www.realsimple.com/work-life/life-strategies/how-to-break-bad-habits [accessed 29 July 2023].

feel the stress building up, or designing your business in a way that reduces the load on you.

- Make goals that will help you to break the habit, such as leaving work earlier each day.

- When you lapse, be kind to yourself; at least you've recognized what's going on and can decide to handle things differently next time.

Alter your expectations

A business owner called Tristan once came to me with a problem. He was an expert in IT infrastructure and had set up a business to advise blue chip companies on their IT systems. There was high demand for his services and he could see that there was the potential for him to grow, but as he put it to me, 'I don't seem to be able to.' I could see that the main issue was his pricing structure. He was charging based on time rather than what his work was worth, and given that scaling would mean he'd need to employ more people, he'd never be able to increase his margins on that basis. Changing the way he charged was a new and scary concept to him, but to his credit he implemented a value-led pricing strategy immediately; given that his fees increased fivefold, it was a courageous move.

Tristan's profits grew in a spectacular fashion, and he ended up employing around a dozen people. However, he now had a new problem: extreme stress. Even though his pipeline was fantastic, his earnings and profits were high and the work the business was doing was universally praised, he couldn't get away from what he saw as the burden of being an employer. He worried about whether he was recruiting the right people and felt a continual responsibility for their job security after they joined him; this made him so miserable that sometimes he didn't want to go into work in the morning.

I asked him whether he thought it was inevitable to feel stressed when running a business, and whether there were alternative ways of doing it. During our discussions, he discovered that while he wanted to earn a good living from his expertise, he didn't really want to build a bigger company. He'd just assumed that he did because it's what other people wanted. After talking it through at length and trying a few different options, he took the decision to reduce his team to between one and three people and create a lifestyle business. He bought a property abroad where he could spend time indulging his passion for surfing and still make really good money, just in an emotionally sustainable way. This was a radical shift, but for Tristan it was the right thing to do. It fundamentally changed his relationship to his company and meant that he stood an excellent chance of never running up an emotional overdraft again.

What expectations do you have of your business? Are they what you really want, or are they what you think you should have? Nikki Gatenby, former MD of digital marketing agency Propellernet, has often spoken about how she only wanted to have a maximum of 60 staff. This meant that when the company employed someone new, that person had to be fantastic because 'seats' were so precious. Her aim was to improve the company's quality and reputation, not simply to grow headcount. Many entrepreneurs are fired up by the idea of growth and hitting target after target; if that's you, then by all means go for it. Just make sure that it's your goal and not somebody else's.

Changing your expectations can also apply when you're in the process of expanding. My client Jenny founded a financial planning consultancy with her associate Geraldine 12 years ago. It started out as a lifestyle business but began to grow rapidly once it became established; this involved having to hire new staff, which they struggled with. Each woman had two young children and, to add to the pressure, Jenny had recently moved out of the city. The original idea for this had been to give her a better work–life balance, but in the short term it meant juggling the demands of the business with settling her children into new schools and building a life in an area where she didn't know anyone. The situation quickly became overwhelming.

In my conversation with her about this, I used the metaphor of a racing car driver who has to take their foot off the accelerator when they go around a corner to avoid skidding off the track. It's only a temporary slowdown, and as soon as the corner has been passed, the car can speed up again. In the same way, while leading a growing business is an exciting and wonderful challenge, you don't have to keep your foot to the floor the whole time. There are times when it makes sense – indeed, it's essential – to tap on the brakes. In Jenny's case, I suggested that she couldn't keep pushing her existing team harder and harder to compensate for the difficulties she was having with recruitment, because it was unsustainable for everyone's emotional overdrafts. This led to her having an honest conversation with a large potential client, in which she said that she and Geraldine needed to defer working with them for another three months because they didn't want to compromise the quality of what they delivered. It was tough for her to do it because she assumed that the client would walk away and not come back, but in fact they were fine with it.

Re-frame your idea of failure

'Don't fear failure. Fear being in the exact same place next year as you are today.' This is an anonymous quote that has resonated with me for a long time, because I've come to the view that much of the reason for people feel stressed is the unacknowledged fear that something terrible will happen if they're not constantly vigilant. 'If I take two weeks off,' they say, 'quality will go down.' Or, 'If I'm not in the office, things don't get done as quickly.' But why? Who else is in charge of quality, or is it only you? And if work isn't done when you're not present, what's the reason for that? Is it the people, the systems or something else that's wrong? Instead of fearing failure, do something about it by putting the right people and processes in place. When you make your business more resilient without you, it means that you don't have to be the one who fixes everything and saves the day. Not only that, it makes the set-up stronger and more sustainable so that you're better able to grow.

Also, what's wrong with failure in any case? We all know that we can learn a lot from it, but somehow we never think that approach applies to us. Pixar, arguably one of the most successful animation businesses of all time, embraces failure. A favourite story of mine from

Ed Catmull's book about the company, *Creativity, Inc.*,[22] is when he tells how the creators of *Toy Story 2* weren't completely happy with the way the movie turned out. This, they realized, was because there were so few failures in the making of it. They hadn't pushed hard enough at the edges of their creativity, so they didn't experience the shortcomings that told them what they were capable of achieving. When Disney bought Pixar, it did so not because it thought it could learn about animation from them (it was Disney, after all), but because it wanted to learn to embrace failure.

Seek help from a coach

In the days when I was running my own businesses, I wish I had seen the value of getting a coach. The role of a coach is to hold up a mirror to your expectations, to allow you to reflect on them and see them for what they are: made-up thoughts rather than reality. They help you to scrutinize your behaviour instead of accepting it as a given.

To a certain extent you can coach yourself, a bit like I suggested earlier when I asked you to question whether you would advise a friend to approach their work like you do. It's a way of stepping outside yourself so that you can interrogate your expectations and assumptions. What alternatives could you explore with this 'friend'? What courses of action would you recommend?

A coach can do more than question and challenge, though. They can also walk alongside you as you develop different

---

[22] Ed Catmull, *Creativity, Inc.: Overcoming the Unseen Forces that Stand in the Way of True Inspiration*, Penguin Random House (2014).

ways of seeing your situation. They have your best interests at heart and will call you out on your unhelpful habits in a gentle and persistent way, which can lead to lasting transformation.

Recharge

I've saved the simplest and most obvious way of changing your expectations around stress for last, which is to regularly find time to unplug and do your 'thing'. Do you remember what you loved doing in your spare time before you started your business? Was there an activity that helped you to re-calibrate? Just as a mobile phone needs to recharge if it's not to run out of juice, so you need to rediscover whatever it is that tops up your resilience levels. It's not weakness to do this; it's just common sense.

The bottom line

- It's a myth that running a business must inevitably be a stressful experience.

- Expecting to feel stressed means that you'll feel that way a lot of the time and that you won't take action to prevent stressful situations arising.

- Methods for changing your expectations around stress are to recognize that you've bought into that myth and then to find ways of changing the habit of stressful thinking.

- You can also re-frame your expectations for your business, accept that failure can be a good thing, seek help from a coach and take time to top up your resilience levels.

10
Duty

'It's my job'
'There's no alternative'
'The buck stops with me'

A FEW YEARS ago, I received a call from a man called Simon, who sounded frustrated about his business. 'I think it might be time for us to work together,' he said. 'Could we meet and have a conversation?' Of course, we could, and during our initial chat he told me about his dilemma.

Five years before, Simon had set up an independent estate agency with five staff. The team did incredible work, the business was profitable and operations ran smoothly. He had three children – one youngster and two teenagers – a wife he adored and (as you would expect with an estate agent) a beautiful house. So, what was the problem? 'Most of us in the company have school-aged children,' he replied. 'So, at half-term there's always a debate about who gets to take the week off. I always insist that my team members go on holiday so they can spend time with their kids, leaving me to cover the office. Every year I promise I'll take half-term off, and every year it's the same. I'd love, just once, to have a whole week to do something fun with my family. It would mean the world to me.'

Resisting the temptation to ask him why he didn't just put himself at the top of the list for a change, I asked him when the last time was that he had taken a break in the school holidays. He sighed miserably. 'It gets worse,' he said. 'A friend invited me to go skiing for three days last half-term, and for once I booked the time off. Unfortunately, the trip had to be cancelled, but rather than spending the time with my children – they seemed happy enough in front of their screens – I ended up spending those days at home on my laptop instead.'

Simon had fallen into the trap that so many leaders do, which is to assume that they always have to be the one who takes the hit. The buck stops with them, so it's their duty to put themselves last when it comes to work satisfaction, personal relaxation and enjoyment of life. And worse, in this case, when Simon did take some time off, his sense of duty meant that he worked rather than unplugging.

What happens when you're ruled by duty

You work late because other people are at their desks and you don't want to seem 'unleaderlike' by going home. You sort out other people's problems because you think you should take responsibility for putting things right. You assume that it has to be you who draws the short straw when it comes to arranging work schedules and holidays, because you're the boss. This is a classic way for you to build up an emotional overdraft.

As Greg McKeown says in his book *Essentialism*, 'If you don't prioritize your life, someone else will.'[23] When you're in constant duty mode, the people you work with will suck everything they can out of you, not because they're vampires but because you've made it easy for them to let you take the hit. Not only that, but they don't have the chance to develop a full sense of responsibility for their own work. You're disempowering them and making life difficult for yourself at the same time.

Being on constant duty is exhausting, but it doesn't have to be that way. How would you feel if you didn't work like this? What would change? Amazingly, when I asked Simon what he thought would happen if he told his staff that this half-term he was going to take the week off, he said, 'You know, they *do* tell me to take half-term off – they're totally up for it and can't understand why I don't. But I still feel like I have to be the one who's here in the office. I just don't know how to stop.'

How to put duty in its rightful place

Of course, all leaders have certain duties and responsibilities, and you're right not to shirk the appropriate ones. But

---

[23] Greg McKeown, *Essentialism: The Disciplined Pursuit of Less*, Crown Business (2014), p. 63.

what I'm talking about here is the blind assumption that the buck has to stop with you on every front, which can lead to you taking on jobs that nobody else wants to do. That's not your responsibility at all. In fact, feeling that it's your duty to do these things is a betrayal of both yourself and the people who work for you. This will become clearer as you work through my suggestions on how to change your attitude to duty, which are:

- Create a personal goal to work towards

- Develop a vision and a plan

- Clarify your role

- Put in place an organizational structure to support your vision

- Challenge your thinking

Create a personal goal to work towards

The first practical step I took with Simon was to talk to him about his personal goal for the business. Setting a goal is important, because if you don't know what direction you're heading in, you won't know how good your decisions are in terms of whether they're helping you to get there. In Simon's case, I asked him to do the five-year letter exercise. This involves projecting yourself five years into the future and writing a letter to your 'today' self. How successful have you been in those five years, and what are the causes of that success? I gave him some time and then asked him to read his letter out to me. He looked a bit uncomfortable but took a deep breath and began. Here's how it went.

Dear Simon (present)

I wouldn't normally be writing a letter about work while I'm on holiday, but I'm making an exception this time because it's five years since I started to change my business. It's been an amazing journey. We're delivering wonderful results for our customers and I've also got to know my family much better than before. I've spent quality time with them and been really present in their lives, which has been by far the most rewarding thing I've ever done. I did say it was going to be a short note because I've got to go and play golf now, so have fun. Good luck.

Love

Simon (future)

I don't know who had more tears in their eyes, him or me. I loved the way that he'd written it as if he was on holiday, because it encapsulated the most important thing that he wanted to change. He didn't write, 'We're making £10 million a year,' or 'I've sold the company and now I can spend time with my family.' Instead, he emphasized the balance he was striking between family and work.

Tucked away in his letter was something else important: *'We're delivering wonderful results for our customers.'* When we explored that nugget, he said, 'I believe that if I hire amazing people and we do high-quality work, the customers will follow. That's how I've built my business over the past five years.' It was true: he'd never marketed his company and his website was out of date, but he still attracted sales because of the incredible work that he and his team did. The act of writing the letter gave him clarity about his personal goal. It became obvious to him that feeling happier with his life was inextricably bound up with being successful in business, and that his aim should be to drive his people to deliver the best possible work so that his estate agency would have quality at the centre of it. This was a company that would deliver for him both as owner and as husband and father.

Do you have a personal goal that helps you to make decisions about what's most important in your business? If you have a guiding light, it makes it possible to stop doing things that aren't contributing towards it and focus your attention on the things that do.

Develop a vision and a plan

Your first and only duty as a leader is not to stay late or to take the rap for everything, but to have a vision and a plan for your business – to set the direction and speed of travel. People want to work for someone who gives them something to get behind – that's how they do their best work. They also need to know how that vision translates to their own roles, otherwise there will be confusion and sub-optimal ways of working. Good people will leave and the mediocre ones will stay; you want amazing staff who are there for the journey, not just for the job.

When you see setting and communicating a vision as your central duty, and know that wasting your energy on being dutiful in non-productive ways means you're less able to do that, your business will thrive. Just as importantly, so will you.

Clarify your role

If you think about it, you have a variety of roles. You're a leader but you also play a part in other people's lives, such as being a mother, father, wife, husband, carer, friend, and so on. Some of the duties you experience in these roles may conflict with one another, and in my conversations with female leaders I often find that women, because of societal pressures and expectations, are particularly prone to the stresses that can be caused by that. Somehow you have to find a way to balance your loyalties to each role so that you don't end up 'betraying yourself' and running up a long-term emotional overdraft.

Creating clarity about your role in the business is the starting point for this, because defining it will help you to see what you should and shouldn't be doing. All those duties you thought you were responsible for can just fall away. You'll go home each day knowing that you did a good job because you're clear on what your role is; you deserve this certainty just as much as everyone else in your organization.

Start by writing a role description. This is different to a job description, which implies a list of tasks; a role description encapsulates a vision and a responsibility for what you do. In my experience, many business owners don't have a role description; nor – unlike their employees – do they have anyone holding them accountable to it. When you start thinking about your leadership role, I hope you'll come up with some key duties, such as to lead, to have a vision, to inspire, to challenge and to create a plan for the business. I'm pretty sure that you won't list one of your duties as being a backstop for everyone else.

While you're writing your role description, there's a helpful exercise that you can do, which I call '20% of your time'. If you're like many leaders, this is how you spend your time:

- 20% on work that currently only you can do in your organization.

- 20% on tasks that are skilled but that other people, if they had the right experience, could also carry out.

- 20% on work that's complex but doesn't require specialist expertise.

- 20% on work that takes a certain amount of ability but could be handled by lots of your staff.

- 20% on stuff that anyone could do but that, for some reason, you seem to pick up.

Now I want you to imagine that you stopped doing that final 20%. Just think – you could double the percentage of time you spend on the tasks that only you can do. That's 40% of your precious time and energy now devoted to your core leadership responsibilities, achieved by eliminating the things that anyone could handle and that you shouldn't be involved with anyway. What would that do for your emotional overdraft?

Put in place an organizational structure to support your vision

Given that your primary duty as a leader is to set and communicate your vision, an organizational structure that supports that vision is essential. It also helps you to scale. I sometimes speak to business owners who say, 'We have a flat structure – we don't like hierarchies. Everyone has their say.' That can work when you're five people, but what happens when you're 10 or more? By that stage you have some staff who are more senior or experienced than others, doing more expensive work, and others who are more junior but still want to grow and develop their careers. People can think it's a bit old-fashioned to have an organization chart, but it's the best way of designing your business so that you do the things you need to do as a leader, not the things you believe you should do. A structure that you keep to is something that will stop you spending your day off wrapping staff Christmas presents, like Anne did.

Seeing how your role fits with others in the company can also give you inspiration for finding ways to remove the final 20% of your workload. Recently, I had a conversation with a guy who would love to spend more time with his family. He was making a great margin on his business, but this was partly down to him handling all the admin himself instead of hiring an assistant. He told me that he thought it was indulgent to bring in a PA – in his words, 'Only jerks have secretaries.' When I asked why he thought that, he replied, 'Well, it's just a status symbol.' Nothing could be further from the truth, I said. When I did the 20% exercise with him, he realized that a huge amount of his time was taken up with tasks that a secretary could handle, and that these were precious hours he could spend with his kids if he chose to.

There are lots of ways that you can restructure who does what if you're imaginative about it. I once had a client who was about to go on a round of fundraising meetings in the US which would involve long drives to cities he wasn't familiar with, and he had loads of work to do as well. I could tell that this was going to be classic emotional overdraft territory for him, so I suggested he hire a driver. 'You can sit in the back of the car and work, and the driver will take the strain of finding the way to the meetings and parking once you're there. You can just turn up, walk in, wow the investors, and walk back out. Then you can carry on with your work.' It might have felt like an indulgence to him to hire a driver, but it was the smart thing to do.

Challenge your thinking

Many years ago, I used to feel that it was my duty to make other people happy, such as my colleagues and family, even if it was at my own expense. This led to me sucking up a lot of unpleasantness and sadness because I thought I was fighting the noble cause of increasing the common happiness pot. Then I started working with a coach. One day, he looked at me quizzically and said, 'What makes you think that there's a finite amount of happiness in the world, so that you have to give away your share in order to make someone else happy?'

This re-framing changed everything for me because it taught me that I could help other people to be happy and be happy myself at the same time; it didn't have to be a trade-off. The barrier standing in my way was my sense of duty, which was making me think that I had to absorb pain to enable others to feel secure and content. When I told my wife about it afterwards, she said, 'All I want is for you to be happy.' I'm sure that's true of the people who care about you as well. Ironically, it can be hard for us to believe that our happiness is something that matters to others, even though we spend our lives trying to make them happy. It's crazy, isn't it?

Sometimes, we'd rather experience the resentment that comes with endless acts of duty than be weighed down by the guilt that comes with abandoning the things we shouldn't be taking responsibility for. But remember, our emotions are the measure of the quality of our thinking. If you're feeling weighed down by duty, at least switch to guilt, because at least then you're getting what you want out of the situation. In time, as you realize the positive benefits to your teams of being less duty-bound, you'll start to feel less guilty in any case.

The bottom line

- Being a leader doesn't mean that you have to solve every problem.

- Thinking that way can cause you to overwork and take responsibility for things that others should be dealing with, which increases your emotional overdraft.

- Structural ways that you can shift your attitude to duty include getting clear about your role, developing a vision for your business and creating an organizational structure that clarifies others' responsibilities.

- Internal ways include setting a personal goal and challenging your assumptions around duty.

11
JFDI

'I get stuff done'
'I'm a doer'

'JUST FLIPPING DO IT' – the favourite phrase of the leader who sees themself as an action-taker or 'doer'. Doers are full of energy and can be decisive leaders; getting stuff done gives them a buzz, and their enthusiasm can be contagious. They know that they're not doing the depth of analysis that others might, but they trust their instincts and love to solve problems by rolling up their sleeves and diving in. When there's a hold-up with a project, they move it forwards. If there's disagreement about which direction to go in, they step in and make a decision. And if something needs to be done but nobody's doing it, they're the one who makes it happen.

So, are you a doer? There's nothing wrong with this way of working when the circumstances warrant it. After all, loving a challenge and rising to it is probably one of the reasons you started a business in the first place. But, if you look a little more closely, you might see that being a doer is often about control; you want to be the one to decide what happens *and* be the person to take action on it. As we explored in the Trust chapter, controlling things can be a key driver for an emotional overdraft, because you can become a workaholic who shoulders too much of the burden. Although in your own mind you're simply mucking in and playing your part, in reality you're making life a lot harder for yourself. Just as importantly, being a doer can become a badge of honour, which means that you ignore other ways of solving problems in favour of your favoured reflex action.

What happens when you see yourself as a doer

As well as being prone to overworking, doers can be difficult to get along with. Ever impatient, they're liable to come across as having a lack of concern for other people's feelings. If you're this way inclined, you probably don't engage as well as you could do in meetings, because while other attendees are talking, you're thinking, 'Can't we just crack on with this?' Brainstorming feels like a drag ('That's it, we've got it, let's not waste any more time') and analyzing a situation is something to avoid. This approach can cause as many problems as it solves because people who *don't* self-identify as doers like you can feel railroaded into making decisions that they're uncomfortable with. Even worse, they can be resentful when their valuable contributions are ignored.

Being a doer might not have been such a problem when you first started your business and needed your can-do energy and risk-taking approach to start the ball rolling. You didn't have a large team to lead so it didn't much matter what other people thought. But when you started building an organization, the art of delegation and allowing people to do their jobs became more important. Today, you haven't quite learnt how to trust people to get on with things, and this is almost certainly more frustrating for them than you realize.

It can also lead to your team members giving up on solving their own problems – after all, what's the point when they know you'll jump in anyway? It's easier to let you take the lead than to feel disempowered when they try to do it themselves. This creates a vicious circle, with them becoming less and less proactive and you feeling more and more annoyed with their passivity: 'I'm the only one who ever does anything around here. People just wait for instructions.' If you look around and find that only a certain sort of person is working for you (the 'tell me what to do' type), this might be the reason.

As a doer, you love to tick tasks off the list because it makes you feel productive. This is sometimes no bad thing, but it can lead to you making ill-informed decisions that would have been improved by a little bit of consideration. You may also be prone to carrying on with a project even when it's heading in the wrong direction, because you don't feel comfortable unless you're taking action. Impulsive and driven behaviour like this can be damaging for your business.

Being a doer can also serve as a habitual relief from the frustration of things not being done quickly enough for your liking, because, for you, the clock is always ticking.[24] By diving in, you give yourself a temporary reprieve from the discomfort of standing on the sidelines and watching events unfold, but it's only a matter of time before the tension builds up again and you have to scratch that itch. You're motivated by the desire to control but, ironically, you've lost control of your own peace of mind. By seeing yourself as a doer, you're working in a perpetual emotional overdraft of your own making.

How to stop being a doer

Spending your time and energy on things that other people should be handling is a difficult habit to shift, because it involves you taking a fresh look at the image you've created for yourself and then learning to lead in a different way. These suggestions will help you:

- Know your badge

- See that being a doer isn't the only way

- Learn to prioritize

- Become comfortable with delegation

- Set up a structure

- Create positive pauses

---

[24] There's a test you can take to see if you're a doer: https://psychologia.co/doer-thinker-quiz [accessed 29 July 2023].

Know your badge

I almost titled this chapter 'Self-image' because being a doer is as much about how we perceive our identity as it is about the way we behave. The badge of doer, however, can be hugely limiting, leading to all kinds of damaging actions and attitudes which increase our own emotional overdrafts and those of our colleagues.

Anne, who you met in a previous chapter, only realized how much of an overwhelming drive she had to get things done when she went through the emotional overdraft monitoring exercise. She discovered that a bad day for her was one in which interruptions from other people, or tech issues, stopped her from accomplishing things, and that she found this disproportionately irritating. She'd never thought of herself as an 'urgent' person but as more of a planner, so this surprised her. Once she recognized that she had an image of herself as being a doer, she was able to find ways of managing her compulsion to take action – for instance, by breaking down long-term projects into more manageable, short-term tasks. This allowed her to feel that she was making progress, which meant that she got less frustrated by the feeling that bigger projects never seemed to be completed. The change in emphasis gave her a lot of satisfaction and helped to reduce her emotional overdraft.

See that being a doer isn't the only way

The All Blacks rugby team in New Zealand has the greatest record of achievements of any sporting team in the world. The secrets of their success are the subject of many studies, but key to it is their 'No Dickheads' policy.[25] They only allow people with a team player mentality to join their ranks, and they empower their senior players by giving them responsibilities on and off the field. They call this 'passing the ball' and, to me, if you see yourself as a doer you're missing an opportunity to foster a similar level of success in your business. You might find collaboration uncomfortable, but to become a better leader you need to respect the perspectives of your colleagues.

There's a theory that people are either thinkers, feelers, or doers. *Psychology Today* has an interesting way of looking at this, and makes some observations about the three approaches.[26] It explains that we tend to create an image of ourselves as being one type or another, and this motivates us to act in ways that reinforce our self-perceptions. 'The Feeler-Self "makes love", the Doer-Self "makes work", and the Thinker-Self makes plans, solves problems, and searches for meaning.'

In fact, we have each personality trait within us to a certain extent, and it's helpful to be on 'friendly terms' with our different selves. The ideal is to be balanced and flexible in the way that you go about things. Sometimes you need to be a doer, but there are times when being a feeler or a thinker is the best option. A great exercise would be to go and 'find' your thinker and feeler in the dark corners of your mind, where they've been neglected for too long. You can also share

---

[25] To me, the definitive book on the All Blacks is James Kerr's *Legacy: What the All Blacks Can Teach Us about the Business of Life*, Constable & Robinson (2013).

[26] See Leon Pomeroy's blog at: www.psychologytoday.com/gb/blog/beyond-good-and-evil/201508/are-you-feeler-doer-or-thinker [accessed 29 July 2023].

your image of yourself as a doer with some of the people you work and live with, and ask how they've experienced it on specific occasions. When you have the answers, reflect on what your intention was at the time. What did you mean the impact of your behaviour to be versus what it felt like to them? This will not only help you to see the effect that your JFDI approach has on others, but also to learn from them about how they like to get things done.

A client of mine, Paul, who saw himself as a doer, was aware that he was annoying his team by constantly jumping in and taking control. I helped him to re-frame the situation by asking him the question: 'What if your strength wasn't to get stuff done, but to help others to "do"?' This stopped him in his tracks, because he realized that he had this superpower of being a doer but wasn't always applying it effectively. As a leader, he should be having conversations with his team about how they did things, especially with those who were predominantly feelers and thinkers. In the end, with his colleagues' permission, Paul became the 'doer coach' in the business. This helped them enormously and, likewise, they started to call him out when he was behaving like a bull in a china shop. His behaviour became a teaching moment for all parties.

Learn to prioritize

Greg McKeown, author of the book *Essentialism* (referenced earlier), points out that doers have 'too many tabs open'.[27]

---

[27] See Greg McKeown's post at: www.linkedin.com/posts/gregmckeown_essentialism-effortless-activity-7011015879270256640-hq3i/ [accessed 29 July 2023].

I know exactly what he means because I'm prone to being a doer myself. If you have this mentality, you're busy but not always productive, making a millimetre of progress on 10 projects rather than focusing your efforts on the most important one. You're gaming the system so that you feel like you're doing stuff, but is it the right stuff? The whirlwind of mental activity that it takes to sustain this for long periods of time is one of the ways that you build up an emotional overdraft.

Being a doer doesn't in itself make you bad at prioritizing. In fact, I've often seen doers sweep aside the trivia to focus successfully on one clear goal; equally, I've seen thinkers become lost in detail, and feelers get bogged down by trying to keep everyone happy. My point is that if you're prone to 'do', you'll often occupy your time with anything in order to feel productive. That's not the same as being impactful or achieving something meaningful, and the uncomfortable feeling that comes with this mismatch between effort and effectiveness (because at some level you know it) can sap your morale.

I love my to-do list (although I call it a 'don't forget' list because it makes me feel as if I own the tasks, rather than the other way around). I also enjoy ticking things off it. But not all ticks are created equal; some jobs are urgent but also disguise themselves as important, and some tasks are important but look like they can wait when they can't. When you're a doer you're always impatient, which is stressful in itself because you're up against the immovable object of time. That means knowing what should be at the top of your list is invaluable. It stops you from cramming too many tasks onto the list, then having to move them from one day to the next because you never seem to get them all done. It's a horrible feeling to go home knowing that you haven't accomplished something you've been intending to do for weeks; far better to focus on what's most important instead.

Being clear on the key priority can be harder than it looks. I had one client, Kasim, who had run his company for 20 years. He was a lovely guy but had a dilemma, which was that he had a new member of staff who was on three months' probation and who wasn't really up to the job. In fact, Kasim had extended his probation already, so this was his final chance. 'Should I sack him?' he asked me. It was obvious that he knew the answer to that already, so my response was to question him on why he was asking me for advice. His reply was that he was dreading hurting the man's feelings because he hated being unkind. This allowed our conversation to go along the lines of what Kasim could do to let his employee go in a kind and supportive way, giving him feedback on his strengths and on the areas he needed to develop. It was likely that the man knew it wasn't working out, and that by being released he'd move somewhere he could thrive. Afterwards, Kasim sent me a text to say that it had gone well and that the man perfectly understood. It's a great example of how not knowing what's truly important can be a huge distraction, stopping you from recognizing what really needs to be done and keeping you up at night for no reason.

Become comfortable with delegation

If you're a doer, you almost certainly have difficulty with delegating. If you find it hard to trust someone else to take responsibility for something, how about putting in place some reporting processes? This can work especially well if one of your staff is prone to being late with delivering. Instead of waiting until the deadline and then feeling frustrated when they haven't completed the task, set them up for success by creating milestones along the way and entering them in both your calendars.

I once worked with a woman called Helen, who was the new MD of a creative agency. She'd been promoted internally and was also quite young, so one of her frustrations was that many people in the business weren't recognizing her authority. Setting milestones for the work she delegated was a game changer for her, and in her case she took it one step further. Instead of putting the follow-up dates in her calendar herself, she asked her staff to enter them in their own and to 'invite' her so that it showed up in hers too. That way, they owned the milestones, and she could forget about the projects until the time came. In the end, she didn't need to carry on doing this for too long as people soon realized that they needed to deliver on time; the requirement wouldn't simply go away by being ignored.

Set up a structure

Successful delegation is tied to people knowing what their roles are and having the authority and autonomy to carry them out. If that's not the case, you'll always end up feeling annoyed with your staff because they won't know where their boundaries lie. This means creating a structure for your organization upon which you can thrive; one that gives you the support you need to be more of a hands-off leader.

A structure will also help your business to go further than you ever thought it could. There's a reason why jellyfish don't rule the world. It's because, unlike prehistoric fish, which had skeletons and could therefore evolve out of the water, jellyfish can only grow to a certain size before they're crushed by their own weight. An accountability framework with clear role descriptions gives you the strength to build bigger and better things. As a doer, you might find structure frustrating and see it as cutting across your desire to reach straight to the heart of what needs to be done. But, actually, it's a liberator, because it means that you won't be constantly hitting a growth ceiling and wondering why your business isn't expanding as much as it could.

Create positive pauses

It's worth asking yourself what you're missing out on when you're a doer. I'd be willing to bet that a key thing is savouring the positive events and lucky chances that come your way (because you never stop doing, right?). As we discussed in Chapter 1, this is an important way of reducing your emotional overdraft, and is easy to overlook because we're hardwired to seek out the negative over the positive. When you lose a client, I bet you pick that apart for months; but, when you win one, how much time do you spend working out why you were successful? Do you rush straight past the experience? In that case, what are you leaving behind?

As I mentioned before, I'm prone to being a doer, and I made this mistake myself only the other day. I'd just finished working with a pair of founders who, after years of being less than effective, had worked out how to divide their responsibilities so that they weren't duplicating effort and treading on each other's toes. It was a powerful result and we were all excited to move forwards. At our next weekly catch-up, I jumped straight in to holding them to account. 'What progress are you making? What's not getting done?' I asked. One of the founders held up a hand and said, 'Could we just stop and recognize what a phenomenal shift happened last week? I'd love us to reflect on it and revel in our success.' She was right – I was rushing past this in my anxiety to get to the 'to-do' list. So, instead of talking about what needed to be done, we had an hour-long conversation in which we explored how the two partners had reached this new realization about the way they worked so that they could tap into that approach more often. It was a fantastic hour, and one that we wouldn't have had if she hadn't made me pause.

The same principle applies for how you spend your free time, which for many doers is quite a scary prospect. How would you feel if you had an empty day arise unexpectedly? Would you still be in your tick-list mentality or could you sit back and relax? It's easy to assume that doing 'nothing' is pointless, but spending time thinking, planning or just enjoying yourself is a legitimate a way to occupy your mind. It recharges your batteries, improves your performance and boosts your resilience.

The bottom line

- When you habitually JFDI, especially in situations where it's not warranted, you can run up an emotional overdraft by putting constant pressure on yourself.

- When you don't delegate, you diminish the people who work for you by demotivating and deskilling them.

- Solutions to the problem of being a compulsive doer include recognizing that it's an image you've chosen to identify with, and learning to do things differently through prioritizing, delegating and pausing.

- You can also learn from how others do things, and put in place structures to support you and help your business to grow.

12
Cost

'We're short of money'
'We don't have the resources'
'I can't justify the expense'

YOU NEED AN extra pair of hands for a project, but you don't have enough budget to draft someone in. Your people are crammed into an office that's too small, but you can't afford a larger space. Your new hires need training, but you put it off until the next financial year so that it doesn't hit your bottom line. These are all examples of decisions that would increase your emotional overdraft, and that of your team, because it feels like it would cost too much to take a different path.

It's especially common to do this when your company is growing and you need to employ more people, or those with specific and expensive skills. In your view, you 'can't afford it', so you carry on doing their work yourself or maybe some of your colleagues divide it up between them. You get by – of course you do. But at the same time, you're borrowing hard on your resilience, and if it goes on for too long you're all going to feel the strain.

A classic example is Jenny, who you met earlier. In the first year of setting up her financial planning consultancy with her associate Geraldine, she pulled most of the weight, as Geraldine had small children who took up a lot of her time. One project involved Jenny spending three weeks away from home, working night and day for a corporate client who had a tight deadline. At the time, she was in her 20s and had no other responsibilities, but she was still so exhausted by it that she developed a sleepwalking habit at the end. She felt as if she had no option but to deliver everything on her own and didn't even consider hiring any help. She just assumed that they couldn't risk the financial burden of bringing in an employee at that early stage.

What happens when you think you can't afford help

Remember the invisible line on the P&L that we talked about in Chapter 1? The one that represents the emotional cost to you and your team of delivering your profits? That's how you 'pay' for not spending money on the help you need. You're using your reserves of resilience to shore up your business because you don't feel able to bring in extra people or use other resources. This means that you, your team or your family are picking up the tab, no matter how much budget you're 'saving'.

So, how does this cost get paid across your business? For you, it's the stress of carrying out work that you're not the most appropriate person for. You might even feel a bit of a fraud, or as if you're getting away with something, because you know that you're not really doing right by your clients. One day, will you be 'found out' and lose them? There's also the opportunity cost of involving yourself, as a leader, in tasks that aren't your remit. Each hour you spend on something that somebody else could do, you're not planning or strategizing, and this erodes your self-worth. It gets worse, because the deeper you sink into an emotional overdraft, the more negative and reactive you tend to become when it comes to decision making. You're on edge, waiting for something bad to happen, and when we expect something to be a certain way it often turns out like that.

Then, what about your teams? Ask yourself what the impact is on that mid-level manager whom you've asked to do things that they wouldn't normally expect to. They might be starting to think that you're holding them back from developing their career, and they're bound to feel overworked and underappreciated. Their emotional overdraft will be increasing by the day. Sometimes this is necessary to plug a short-term gap, but it shouldn't be a constant condition.

Finally, let's look at the impact on your family. If you're running up an emotional overdraft at work, they'll be paying some of the price at home. You won't be contributing as much as you should to their wellbeing; nor will you be looking after yourself. Maybe you've stopped going to the gym because you don't have time, which makes you grumpy and hard to get along with. It's easy to overlook this aspect (and I've done it myself in the past), but when we think that we can't afford to make things easier for ourselves at work it inevitably spills over into our home lives. Let's not kid ourselves that there's no cost attached for the people we love the most.

How to find the resources you need

The cost driver of an emotional overdraft is an unusual one in that it appears to come from outside ourselves, and to be fixed and intransigent. We either have enough resources to make our working lives easier or we don't – right? However, it also has traits in common with the urgency driver, which, as we explored in Chapter 8, has as much to do with the way we see a situation as it does with the reality of it. In addition to that, there are plenty of options when it comes to using the resources you have more effectively. Here are some suggestions for how you can reinvent the notion of cost being a reason for building up an emotional overdraft:

- Question your assumptions

- Have accurate management information

- Change what you charge

- Work out what's most important

- See hiring as a way to grow

- Protect your own wages

Question your assumptions

I had a client called James who ran an incredibly profitable marketing business. In one of his sessions with me, he told me that he'd spent all his Christmas holidays worrying about whether his plans for the following year were going to be scuppered because the company had recently lost £300,000-worth of revenue. 'We're going to have to stop hiring, Andy,' he said, 'and focus on new business instead.' I imagine you might think the same way if you were in his shoes; it seems like the obvious solution. But when I asked him how much new business he already had in the pipeline, he said, 'Oh, I'm not sure. I haven't added it up.' It turned out that he had £500,000-worth of new revenue due in for the coming year, either from new clients yet to come fully onboard or from existing clients who were spending more. In fact, in the first two months, he had £200,000-worth more work to deliver than at the same time last year.

This shows how, when we feel panicked, we automatically focus on the negative and ignore the opportunities under our noses. If James had put the brakes on hiring more people, he'd not have had the resources to service the new work that was already in the pipeline – let alone deal with anything that came as a result of his new business efforts. And the crazy thing was, he couldn't see it. Normally a level-headed person, he'd sent himself into a tailspin because he was only looking at the 'bad' data rather than at the balanced picture. This also illustrates how 'we can't afford it' is sometimes a question of perception. Often, we do have the money, but we've decided to spend it on things that won't reduce our emotional overdrafts. I'll explore this notion further below.

Have accurate management information

The only reason that James was able reliably to question his assumptions about the coming year's revenue was because his pipeline data was accurate and up to date. If you're convinced that you can't afford more help, you need to know what's going on in your business. Imagine driving a car without a working speedometer. If you wanted to make sure that you weren't pulled over by the police, you'd have to travel at a consistently slow speed to be on the safe side. In the same way, if you don't have high-quality management information, you won't know how fast to push your business. This will result in you making decisions which increase your emotional overdraft, such as assuming that you don't have enough resources for more people, or misunderstanding how much work you can give the ones you have. In fact, you can drive quite close to the limit if you have accurate intelligence. Just as a speedometer tells you that you're doing 69 in a 70 limit, so your data inform you about what you can and can't do.

A surprising number of leaders have inaccurate management information, or, if they do have good numbers, they're out of date. If this is you, one of the most important things you can do to reduce your emotional overdraft is to make sure that you have a realistic picture of what's going on in your business, including what's coming up. Once you know what you're dealing with, the self-delusion ends because there's no arguing with the facts. And if you're wondering how you're going to achieve this, a part-time financial director can be a great asset. Many of my clients have such a person come in for a day or two a week to take charge of their numbers, and they consider it to be money well spent. It might reduce their short-term profitability to hire that person, but they're repaid in the reduction of their emotional overdrafts and the business opportunities it presents. Only this week, I visited a client with an FD I know, to go through the client's numbers. In one hour, we'd stripped away masses of noise and irrelevance to reveal a set of basic management information that was clear and easy to follow. This was a revelation to my client, who then started drawing impactful conclusions and asking probing questions, all of which helped to move his business forwards.

Change what you charge

'Okay, so this gets me so far', you may be saying. 'But what if I just don't have the money to hire an extra person? I can't magic it out of thin air.' To that I'd say, 'Are you charging your clients for them?' More often than not, the need to hire experienced or senior people comes from leaders expanding their businesses by adding more specialized services to the generalized ones they started with. The problem is that they often don't charge their clients extra for the benefit.

If this is the case for you, your first step is to check that the specialist service you're providing is what your clients genuinely want. If it is, then you need to speak to your clients about charging for it. If their response is to say that they don't want to pay then they clearly don't value the service, so don't supply it to them – your workload problem is now solved. If they say they do want it and they're prepared to pay, then rethink your charging structure so that you have the resources to hire the extra personnel. It's also a good idea to label the new service so that the need it addresses is clear; that way, you can sell it to other clients as well.

Work out what's most important

A client of mine, Gillian, ran a business with around 25 staff. The workload was expanding and she was in need of more people, but was worried that it would be too financially stretching. We did a calculation based on how the staff were being utilized and unearthed some surprises: it turned out that she had the equivalent of six people who were doing 'nothing'. Of course, they were working hard, but the tasks they were carrying out weren't contributing to the business in the most effective way. Although Gillian was a bit shocked to discover this piece of management intelligence, at least it gave her a lever to pull.

Her next step was to make some decisions. Two of the people were employed in legacy roles which clients weren't paying for; not only was this wasteful but it was also demoralizing for the staff involved, as they knew that their work wasn't being valued. Unfortunately, there was no option but to let them go, but Gillian helped them to find other jobs and gave them a lot of support. Two further people had the talent and ability to do more but were being underutilized, so they were redeployed. The final two people weren't actually whole people but an aggregation of time that added up to the equivalent. Gillian took these 'people' and re-allocated their hours across the company where there was a need for it, such as to a couple of important internal projects that had been languishing for lack of attention. The net impact across the business was a reduction in everyone's emotional overdrafts, because not only did it release funds to hire more people, but the staff that Gillian had redeployed were now doing work that felt meaningful and worthwhile. For her, it was as if she'd found six extra employees hiding in a corner of the office.

You can do a similar exercise. I suggest creating a staff grid, with potential on the y-axis and impact on the x-axis, as in Figure 4. Plot everyone in the business onto the four boxes so that you can see who's low or high impact and who's low or high potential. In the top right you have high potential/high impact; these are people you want to keep and nurture. Below them is high impact/low potential; you have to make a decision about those. To the left of them is low impact/low potential; you know what to do with them. And then there are the high potential/low impact people who may need attention. In Gillian's case, she realized that she had a lot of people in the top left, in the high potential/low impact square. This told her that she needed to dedicate more time to training and development because, although the company had done a great job of hiring the talent, this wasn't having enough of an effect on the business.

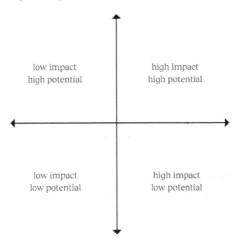

Figure 4   *The potential/impact grid*

Being clear on your priorities can work wonders for your emotional overdraft in another way, too, which is to help you decide what work to focus on. This stops you (and everyone else) from feeling overwhelmed. There's an exercise for this that I've undertaken hundreds of times, both in my own businesses and those of my clients, and it works brilliantly every time. All you need is a whiteboard and your team gathered together in one place. On the whiteboard, list between you all of the short-term activities in your business plan. Leave nothing off. Then, give each team member between three and five red dot stickers, and ask them to put them beside the items they think are the business's highest priorities. The idea is not for them to take turns, but to decide in advance and then do it together so that they're not being influenced by one another. If they want to, they can put all their dots beside one task, or they can spread them out more evenly.

The result will look a bit like an attack of the measles, but there will also be clumps of dots around selected activities. It's an excellent way of helping people to prioritize what's most important, because you'll find that a chunk of tasks on the list can now be abandoned, and what's left has everyone's commitment. A workload that was previously chaotic and unmanageable is now streamlined and doable. I can guarantee you that, the night after you've done this exercise, you'll sleep like a baby.

See hiring as a way to grow

James, the marketing company founder I mentioned earlier, used to be a classic business hoarder, in that his instinct was always to spend as little as he could. The way he saw it, any surplus revenue should be squirrelled away in case it was needed for an emergency. Eventually, I managed to persuade him that his profits were fuel for growth. I explained that not investing in more staff, or on training the staff he had, was like planting a tree in a tiny pot. He'd end up with a perfect-looking bonsai, but it would be tiny and constricted.

It can feel scary to spend money in this way, but it will put your team under pressure if you don't. And it's important to do it properly. Once James could see that he had a future work requirement that would need people to service it, he knew that he had to structure his organization so the new hires would be in the right seats. It also meant that he took a temporary hit on profitability. However, because his existing staff weren't put under intolerable pressure as a result of the new recruitment, the good people stayed and everyone contributed to the amazing year they ended up having.

Protect your own wages

In the first business I owned, I had an investor who was older and more experienced than me. The company was going through a fast-growth phase and cash flow was tight, so I had a conversation with him about how we could cope with this. One of my proposals was that I cut my own salary. 'I don't recommend doing that,' he said. 'You'll give yourself stress at home, it will have an impact on your family, and instead of relaxing in the evenings you'll be worrying about how you can afford what you need.' These were wise words. What he was effectively saying was that saving money like this would mean that I'd be paying the price through my emotional overdraft. Equally, my family would be paying for it out of theirs – it would have been a false economy.

Of course, taking a temporary salary cut can sometimes be the right thing to do, but only if you're confident that cash will start flowing into the business at a later date. You can then repay yourself with a bonus when it does. The problem comes when it's a knee-jerk reaction to a business problem, or when you never pay yourself enough through force of habit. I once worked with Amina, a woman who only paid herself half of what she should have done, even though her business had a healthy balance sheet. 'That's the nature of running your own business,' she said. 'The owner comes last.' As you'll understand by now, she was subsidizing her company by dipping into her resilience, because her small salary was stopping her doing a lot of the things that she wanted. After some benchmarking on what MDs get paid, we agreed to meet somewhere between what she was paying herself and what I thought she should be, and it made a significant difference to her wellbeing. She stopped feeling resentful and started enjoying her life more.

The bottom line

- Thinking that you can't afford to bring in extra people or resources is a key reason for doing work that you shouldn't.

- All you're doing is to push the 'cost' somewhere else – either onto your own emotional overdraft or onto that of your staff and family.

- There are many ways to create funding that don't seem obvious at first.

  - Some are based on how you think, such as challenging your assumptions, interrogating your priorities and seeing hiring as an investment in future growth.

  - Others are based on external factors, such as making sure that you have high-quality management intelligence and altering your charging structure.

13
At a Loss

'I'm out of ideas'
'I've no other solution'

SO OFTEN, WHEN we're in the thick of things, we act on autopilot and leap to the most obvious solution because we can't think of any other option. Maybe we don't even consider the idea that there are alternatives to what we've come up with. Unfortunately, the choices we make when we behave like this are often the ones that heap more stress on us and increase our emotional overdrafts.

What happens when you act on autopilot

When you're operating under pressure and drawing hard on your resilience, it's even more difficult than usual to see the big picture. You're hoping that dealing with this or that problem will magically make everything all right, when you know deep down that it won't. It's as if you're hacking your way through a jungle, focusing only on what's in front of you instead of understanding what overall direction you're heading in. Not only does this increase your emotional overdraft, it's also never the optimal way to come up with new ideas or solutions that work.

This is when it's easy to start being critical of yourself, which – ironically – makes you feel even worse. Mira, who you met previously, found this when she was going through an extra-busy period. She realized that the hours she was devoting to her business were coming out of other things that mattered to her – sleep, spending time with her husband, keeping in touch with friends – and that, somehow, she'd managed to get her priorities the wrong way around. This made her feel like a failure because she couldn't escape the conclusion that she'd brought it on herself. The problem was that she didn't know what to do about it because it seemed like there was no alternative if she was to have a successful business.

How to come up with alternative ideas

It seems like an unsolvable conundrum: if you haven't any idea of what else to do, then what on earth can you do? And, yet, logic alone says that there's always an alternative way. The challenge you have is that, given the way humans think in stressful situations, it feels real to you to assume that there's no choice but to take the stressful or demanding course of action. That's why you need ways of raising yourself up out of the undergrowth so you can see what the other options are. Here are some suggestions for how to do that:

- Ask around

- Create a personal board

- Recognize and challenge negative self-talk

- Focus on your learning

- Re-frame the problem

Ask around

If you're anything like me, you've often looked back on a decision that you made in a difficult situation and, in the calm after the storm, realized it wasn't the best one you could have chosen. It's partly for this reason that asking other people for their opinions can be so valuable, because they're not hacking through the jungle with a machete like you are – their thinking is clearer and their emotions are calmer than yours. The best thing about this is that, even though you're the leader, you *don't have to know* what all the alternatives are; in fact, it's not even reasonable to expect that of yourself. The only thing that's 'on you' is to develop your business. There are people in your team who have different expertise and life experience to you and that might lead them to come to alternative conclusions. They're a resource waiting to be tapped. Maybe they can give you ideas, or even, just through conversing with you, spark something that would lead you to come up with your own alternatives.

Recently, I attended a board meeting for one of my clients and we all headed out for dinner afterwards. On the way to the restaurant there was much conversation about some complex plans that were afoot for developing the business, involving an acquisition, some changes to the team, new office and many other moving parts. The MD started firing off questions, clearly jumping from one thought to the next. Rather than answer them, I asked him to be present and let his subconscious do the heavy lifting. Things would settle. He took my advice and had an enjoyable and relaxing meal. Then, just as the desserts were being served, he sat bolt upright and grabbed a napkin from the table next to him. He scribbled a diagram and stared at it. 'That's it!' he said. 'That's how it fits together.' By listening to my suggestion to stop churning over the issue and give it room, he unlocked his ideas. I told him to keep the napkin and frame it as part of his business story.

The most successful businesses are those in which leaders don't see themselves as the only person responsible for coming up with solutions. In fact, they actively recruit colleagues who think differently to them and each other, and who are in a position to spot ways forward that others haven't thought of. This is what I call diversity of thinking, and it's something that those leaders have made a deliberate decision to do; they also encourage their team to push back on their decisions when necessary.

It's not only your colleagues who can give you a different perspective, but also professional groups outside of work. I'm in a guild group with Guild.co, which is a networking platform made up of private, work-related groups. It's a place where I can ask questions about something that's troubling me and receive helpful answers from people who know where I'm coming from. There are other places where you can do this as well, such as LinkedIn. I guarantee you that, when you arrive at your next 'no idea' moment, there will be people in your industry who have been in your shoes and are willing to chip in. My suggestion is that you start tapping into these networks now, and contribute before you ask for advice because you're more likely to receive a warm reception if you're already seen as a helper. There's an added benefit to this as well, which is that by helping someone whose problem you're not wrapped up in, you may come up with new solutions to your own issues. It sounds counter-intuitive, but it works.

Finally, there's comfort in knowing that you're not the only person with problems and no idea how to solve them. This on its own can help to lessen your emotional overdraft. It will also make you less likely to lean on your team or your family, because some matters are best not shared with those whom you work or live with. It's always useful to know where else to turn.

Create a personal board

A more formalized way of doing what I've talked about above is to create what's called a personal board. This is a group of people you can call when you're faced with day-to-day decisions, crossroads and challenges, or to have as a listening ear when you sense that the direction you're heading in will increase your emotional overdraft but you don't know what else to do. The people on your board don't necessarily need to know that they're on it, but they should have time for you, respect you, be willing to listen and also be genuinely interested in seeing you succeed.

I see a personal board as being made up of six seats: a *cheerleader*, who inspires you with fresh ideas and motivates you to make a difference; a *career coach*, who helps you to work out what to do and how; a *connector*, who can introduce you to others in your profession or industry and broaden your network; a *peer*, who listens to you vent and helps you to get back on track; a *mentor*, who's experienced and offers you guidance and advice; and, finally, a *wellness coach*, who encourages you to look after your health and wellbeing.

The beauty of a personal board is that it gives you a support structure when you're lost for ideas. It also ensures that there's a balance to the advice you receive, because you're asking for it from a designated range of people. They're the ones who can help you to quiet the noise and see a way forward, so that you're not stuck in the same old emotional overdraft rut. Don't be shy with your board – make use of them. If they're happy to be leaned on, lean in; it's easy to underestimate how rewarding it is to be there for someone else.

Recognize and challenge negative self-talk

'I run this company – I should be able to sort this out.'

'I shouldn't have left it this long. Why didn't I deal with it before?'

'I knew it – I should have hired better people. Why do I always make the same mistake?'

'I should have spoken to that client about this weeks ago – I'm an idiot.'

The heartless way we talk to ourselves when we can't think of how to solve a problem is incredible. We'd never dream of saying these things to a friend or colleague (or at least, I hope we wouldn't). And if someone said them to us, we'd probably think they were a horrible bully. It's extremely unhelpful to beat ourselves up about everyday mistakes and oversights, not only because it raises our emotional overdrafts but also because it layers more negative thoughts on top of the ones we already have. Our judgement becomes ever more clouded as we kick ourselves for being so 'stupid' or 'forgetful', which makes it harder for us to have a clear-eyed view of what should be done. In the business world, there are plenty of people who are willing to beat us up and bring us down, so let's not join the queue and finish the job ourselves.

This is all very easy to say, but not so simple to put into practice.[28] I find that an instant way of spotting that I'm talking myself down is to be aware of when I use the word 'should'. It acts as a trigger for me to pause and check my thoughts. You may recognize these kinds of phrases coming up for you:

'I should exercise every day.'

'I should be more patient with people.'

'I should be more positive.'

It's not that the intention behind the words is wrong; it's the sense of obligation that comes with 'should'. It can

---

[28] See: www.healthline.com/health/mental-health/stop-automatic-negative-thoughts [accessed 29 July 2023].

set off a train of guilty thoughts and leave you feeling powerless and defeated. Try using 'could' instead.

'I could exercise every day.'

'I could be more patient with people.'

'I could be more positive.'

Can you feel the difference?

When you've identified your negative thoughts, you can also put them on trial. Is there any evidence to support this terrible view of yourself? For instance, you've left a client presentation until the last minute and you find yourself thinking: 'I should have done this earlier. I'm so disorganized. When will I learn? Now it's going to bomb because I don't have enough time to prepare. How on earth will we win the pitch?' Ask yourself where the evidence is for these judgements. Yes, you could have been better prepared, but you're not always this disorganized. And, yes, you're not giving yourself the best chance of success by rushing the presentation, but you've performed well in these situations in the past. You're only doing your best, which is all that anyone can do.

Focus on your learning

If you've been running your organization for a while, it's likely that you haven't undertaken any active learning or training for some time. You're so busy putting what you've learnt in the past into practice that you may have lost some of the curiosity that you once had. It's probably because you think you don't have time but, from an emotional overdrive perspective, learning can be an invigorating thing to do. We humans thrive on it – we're made to learn – and if we stop, we can find it harder to see new solutions or come up with fresh ideas.

Learning can take many forms. It can be formal courses, networking, asking questions of people and also 'on the job' training such as when you analyze things that have gone wrong or even undertake some simple self-reflection. Failure simply means that you're pushing at the boundaries of what you can do, so the next time you find yourself giving yourself a hard time, how about asking yourself (and your team) what you can learn from it? Are there systems and processes that could be altered to prevent it from re-occurring? This in itself helps you to reduce your emotional overdraft, because when you take something constructive from a difficult situation it makes you feel empowered.

When you feel yourself stuck for a way forward, stop and breathe for a second. If you could learn something new right now, what would be the one insight that would help you with your business? A classic example that raises itself with many leaders is understanding their financials. They've learnt about them from their accountants, or picked up knowledge here and there, but they don't feel confident about their numbers. There's a lot of jargon around accounting – I'll be honest: I spent years trying to remember the difference between a debit and a credit – and yet I can now understand a profit and loss statement because I've gone through some training. If there's anything that you need to fix, you can definitely spare a day to do it; you might even enjoy it or realize that you know more than you think you do. If you could just add hot water and gain an instant skill (I call it 'Pot Noodle learning'), what would you focus on?

A favourite saying of my father's, which I heard all the time when I was growing up, is 'Where there's muck, there's brass'. All the stress that you're dealing with (the muck) can be instantly converted into positive emotions (brass). Something that was, minutes ago, painful and frustrating, now becomes liberating and stimulating – it's like alchemy. Jenny, realized this when she did her emotional overdraft monitoring. She saw that it was important for her to seek out learning experiences as a way of boosting her resilience levels. In her case, she went on a leadership camp, which she found hugely inspiring, and committed to investing in her own learning going forward. She saw it not only as a way of becoming a more effective leader but also as a method for topping up her emotional overdraft.

Re-frame the problem

Sometimes the old stories are the best. In the early 1900s, two travelling salesmen were given the task of selling shoes in a faraway market. A few days after they arrived, each sent a telegram back. One said: 'Terrible news! Nobody here wears shoes.' The other said: 'Brilliant opportunity! Nobody here has any shoes yet.'

This is a classic example of a re-frame, or choosing to look at a problem (or should that be an opportunity?) in a new light. If you want to change something, be it how you feel, how you do things or what you believe, it always begins with you directing your thoughts into a different reality. In the same way, I often use re-framing when I'm challenging clients to solve problems. People fear change, so instead of telling them, 'We need to change this business', I re-frame the question as, 'What do you think would make this the perfect organization?' People are never short of ideas, and a simple re-frame can make all the difference as to whether you stay stuck in an 'I'm at a loss' syndrome or are liberated by the introduction of new options.

If you feel like there's no choice but to take the most mentally or emotionally taxing route, try asking yourself the following questions:

'What would I do if I had one more hour?'

'What would I do if I had one more pound or dollar?'

Now you're no longer focusing on how to get more things done in less time, but how to get fewer things done which are of greater importance in the time (or with the money) available. It's as if you've given yourself a superpower.

Like all change, getting into the habit of re-framing takes practice. The more you do it, and the more you involve other people in it, the more that a wide variety of solutions will open up to you. In time, you'll start to see that there are alternatives where you thought there were none, and that many of them will be helpful for both your business and your own wellbeing.

The bottom line

- Assuming that there's no other way of doing something represents an acceptance of self-limiting thinking.

- This creates a snowball effect, in which you can't see a way out of your situation so you become even more stressed and even less resilient than you were before.

- Ways of solving this problem often rest with other people, so asking them for ideas and creating a personal board are a huge help.

- You can also address your inner habits by talking to yourself in a more positive way, focusing on your learning and getting into the habit of re-framing your knotty problems.

14
Load-balancing

'I have a short-term need'
'I'm stepping in to fill a gap'

YOU KNOW HOW it is. You start your day with the best of intentions, but then something unexpected or urgent crops up and you find yourself short of spare hands to deal with it. Who steps in to plug the gap? You do. The task might be nothing to do with your leadership role, but someone has to save the day and – given that nobody else is available and you're the person in charge – it's you.

Naturally, there are times when it's legitimate to act as 'burst capacity' in this way; it's not a bad thing to put something less pressing onto the back burner if it means you can avert a disaster. The problem is when it becomes a habit, and you constantly find yourself struggling to do the work that you should be doing because you're stepping into other people's jobs. That's when it contributes towards your emotional overdraft.

What happens when you turn yourself into a load-balancer

Saving the day can be addictive – it's exciting and can make you feel needed. But think about what it's doing to your stress levels. While you're putting out the fire in front of you, other fires may be flickering elsewhere, in danger of getting out of control. The review session that you were going to have with your finance head is cancelled; the time that you'd set aside this afternoon to research your competitors is junked; a meeting with an important client, which you'd planned to attend, is now shoved onto to a junior member of staff. You know that you're not dealing with these things, and it bothers you, but you don't have the time to do anything about them because you're focused on the urgent matter in hand. Then the self-doubt about your leadership skills creeps in: 'How did we get to this? Why didn't we predict it was going to happen? Have I hired the wrong people? Are we just terrible at planning?' Thought by insidious thought, your emotional overdraft rises to unsustainable levels and eats away at your peace of mind.

It's not only you who's affected by this. When you step in to balance the workload, it can feel humiliating and undermining for other members of your team. If it's one of them who's responsible for causing the problem you're solving, they don't have the chance to fix it. And what will happen next time there's an emergency? Will they expect you to plug the gap once more? You're setting yourself up for a cycle of frustration in which you're discouraging people from being proactive, then feeling annoyed with them because they're waiting to be told what to do.

This compounding of pressure can have a serious impact on your resilience, which in turn affects your ability to make rational decisions about who should do what. So, you put yourself in a position where you're always taking impulsive action instead of thinking things through. The further you slide into emotional debt, the more dangerous this can be.

How to stop being a load-balancer

As a leader, it's your job to look ahead, not to mend the holes in the road in front of you. It can be a challenge to change your habits, but the good news is that if you can find a way to focus solely on leadership, most of the problems associated with load-balancing will go away. Here are some methods for achieving this:

- Set up processes to prevent repeatable problems

- Avoid over-servicing your clients

- Label your behaviour

Set up processes to prevent repeatable problems

If a crisis keeps repeating itself, it's worth spending time creating a process that prevents it arising in the first place, and training people to follow it. That's your real responsibility as a leader. For instance, if you can predict that your clients give you crazy amounts of work in December because they shut down for Christmas and want to clear their decks, there are procedures you can put in place to cope with this. You might not allow your staff to take holidays in the first half of December, or you could plan other projects around that time period so that they don't clash.

Processes also prevent self-generated problems arising. Suppose one of your clients is giving a career-defining presentation at an important conference, and the materials you're supplying for him aren't ready on time. There's no one else available, so you step into the breach. Cursing under your breath about why you have to save the day yet again, you work all evening and, in the rush, make some spelling mistakes on the slides. Your client is humiliated in front of his audience and is understandably furious with you, threatening to withhold payment on the project. Now, we're all human and sometimes this kind of thing happens, but usually there are ways of avoiding it. What are your procedures for checking materials that go out? How about having an internal deadline that gives you time for that checking process? Could you have insisted that the client got involved earlier and give you feedback in a timely manner?

In other words, when a situation is going pear-shaped, your first question shouldn't be, 'How can I sort it out?' but 'How can I design it better?' This will help to reduce your emotional overdraft, not only because you'll have fewer load-balancing demands in the first place, but also because you'll be creating a positive out of a negative. It's as if you've installed a sprinkler system to damp down a fire before it becomes a raging inferno.

Some people load-balance all the time. One of my clients, Nigel, used to fly three times a week to see clients in Europe. In one of our sessions, I asked him why he was doing it and he said, 'It's a pain, but the team is really stretched. The client's an important one so I'm stepping in to do it.' It turned out that the task was strictly operational and nothing to do with his leadership role; a junior person could easily handle it. 'Have a think about this,' I replied. 'Because you're flying abroad three times a week, it means that there are many things on our coaching list that won't get done. You'll be tired and stressed from the travelling and you're going to end up resenting the time and energy it takes. Surely there are better alternatives, right?' Having given it some thought, Nigel came to the realization that his job as leader was to anticipate the work volume and hire the right people to handle it. That was a far more efficient use of company expenditure than him doing the work himself. He'd thought he was being helpful by load-balancing but in fact he was harming his business and increasing his emotional overdraft.

Avoid over-servicing your clients

I imagine that you originally set up your company because you had a service that you were excellent at delivering, and that clients wanted and were prepared to pay for. That's a sound basis for a business. However, some clients are more profitable than others. If you have a demanding one who asks you to spend a lot more time on their account than they're paying for, it's easy to say yes – you want to keep them happy, after all. But you have to remember that somebody, somewhere, is paying the price, and if you're filling the work gaps yourself, it's you.

There are two options in this type of situation. One is to say no to the client, or to manage their expectations more carefully. That involves you training your account managers to understand that servicing a client doesn't mean saying yes to everything, and to draw boundaries in a way that doesn't damage the relationship. The other option is to charge the client more and hire extra people to do the work. Either way, you're in control and your emotional overdraft remains unaffected.

Some businesses hardly ever operate in fire-fighting mode, the reason being that they hire the right quality people and charge their time fully. They also have rigorous processes. I once worked in an advertising agency that invested heavily in recruitment, onboarding and training. New hires became productive quickly, and because the agency's processes were slick and everyone knew how to follow them, projects ran like clockwork. I never saw any of that company's leaders jumping in to help out with something that was getting out of hand.

There are always freelancers, as well. Business owners often object to them because they think they're expensive, and it's true, they do cost more than permanent employees on a pro rata basis. But you're not paying for their pensions, their holidays or their equipment. And how much more expensive is it for you not to take advantage of what they offer, both in terms of your emotional overdraft and the opportunity cost to your business? Unlike the figure on the invoice that the freelancer hands you, it's difficult to quantify those other costs, so it's easy not to give them the same level of attention. In most cases, a freelancer is the intelligent option if you have a short-term gap to fill.

This all assumes, of course, that you're aware of the imbalance between client revenues and work levels in the first place. Are your staff filling in timesheets? Do you understand whether you're utilizing your people in the most efficient way? Do you have a target utilization per individual so that you can calculate your productive capacity? When you have the facts, you're in a good position to decide what to do about your demanding clients. Whatever decision you take, don't just absorb the cost yourself by stepping in to balance the load when needed. That only propagates the problem.

Label your behaviour

Because stepping in to do things that aren't in your remit can be such an automatic process, it's helpful to give it a name. Labelling allows you to recognize it when it's happening, which is the first step to putting a stop to it. You could call it 'Stepping in' or 'Just this once' or – my favourite – 'Being a mayfly' (because mayflies only live for one day, and it's easy to tell yourself that you'll do it today and then never again). A name gives your colleagues something to refer to: 'Hang on, are you being a mayfly?' or 'Just "stepping in" again are you, John?' This will give you pause and allow you to assess whether you being involved is really the best option. It also brings a touch of humour into the situation, which is never a bad thing. Your emotional overdraft will thank you for it.

The bottom line

- Stepping in to load-balance might look like strong leadership but it's usually a result of a lack of planning and control.

- When you do this, you put pressure on yourself, neglect other areas of your business and demotivate your staff.

- Sound processes and planning are at the heart of avoiding the problem arising in the first place.

- Avoiding over-servicing your clients and giving your behaviour a name are other tools to use.

15
Empathy

'I'm part of the team'
'I'm showing care and commitment'
'I feel guilty if I don't'

MANY YEARS AGO, I started a new job at an advertising agency and was thrilled when the CEO told me that he'd hired me because he was impressed with my empathy. I thought it was one of the loveliest things that anyone had ever said to me. And it's true, empathy is generally a good thing, but it can also be a significant driver for your emotional overdraft if you misapply it or it's generated by the wrong thinking. When you feel guilty if you don't help people out, or when you get sucked into their problems at the expense of your own wellbeing, having empathy for your team can have a negative impact on your resilience. As organizational psychologist Nicole Lipkin says in her article, 'The Good, Bad and Ugly of Empathy', 'If a leader were to absorb the collective emotions of their employees, it would be extremely difficult to get out of bed in the morning, never mind lead a company.'[29] I can't think of a better way to describe the impact of misapplied empathy than that.

What happens when you misunderstand empathy

Just to reiterate: there's nothing wrong with being empathetic. In fact, leaders should definitely be kind – it's a great quality to have. But when empathy springs from a need to be liked or a yearning to belong, that's when it starts to be at your own expense. You try to keep everyone happy; you don't want anyone to think badly of you; you strive to be the person who bonds the team together. Then, one day, you overhear someone in the staff kitchen saying something negative about you, or you see a comment in an email that makes you feel crushed. I can guarantee that your staff don't feel responsible for your happiness in the way that you do for theirs, and if your sense of personal satisfaction in your business is dependent on what people think about you, you're laying yourself open to serious disappointment. It's fine to have an emotional connection with your colleagues, but if it's a proxy for closeness to people outside of work, it represents a cost to you.

---

[29] Nicole Lipkin, 'The Good, Bad and Ugly of Empathy', *Forbes*, 8 March (2022). Available at: www.forbes.com/sites/nicolelipkin/2022/03/08/the-good-bad-and-ugly-of-empathy [accessed 29 July 2023].

What can appear to be empathy on the surface is often neediness. I know founders who've told me that they resent employees who leave to go on to other jobs. This makes no sense. If someone resigns, you should want them to go forth on great terms with you, and as advocates for your business. True empathy would be to feel delighted for them, and proud that they learnt so much from you that they're able to move on to better things. It's emotionally costly for you to be clinging on to the idea that people work for you because they need you as much as you need them.

Misapplying empathy also stops you being an effective leader. When you do something because you feel you should do it, such as work late because other people are still at their desks and you want to be supportive, you're not helping them. Ironically, they may be desperate to go home but don't think they can because you're still there. What they really want is direction. People can handle all sorts of pressure if they know that it's taking them towards an important goal; your primary responsibility is to make clear what that goal is. When you sacrifice leadership to be 'one of the gang', that's to do with your ego and not your empathy.

Some of the female leaders I work with make the point that women are expected to be more empathetic than men. There's a societal conditioning that women are nurturers and carers, and this spills over into the workplace, where it's assumed they'll be supportive of others. This also goes for the way that women have told me they combine their business and personal lives. Mira puts it like this: 'If everybody else is okay, I'm okay, and vice versa. I see moods as clouds that we carry around with us, and that other people breathe in. I'm hugely affected by other people's emotional overdrafts.' This is an extra burden to carry, and can be hugely draining if it continues long term.

How to gain a better understanding of empathy

To understand a person, walk a mile in their shoes. And if you don't like that person, it's okay – you're a mile away and you still have their shoes. I love this joke, but more seriously, though, learning how to handle empathy in ways that don't drain your resilience comes down to understanding the thought processes behind it. Your thinking creates your feelings, which drive your behaviour, which in turn affects the outcomes you achieve. If your thinking about empathy is off kilter, it will cause you to behave in a way that you assume is empathetic but isn't, and the effect that you then have on others, and on yourself, won't be what you intend. Here are some different ways of looking at empathy:

- Understand how empathy and leadership work together

- Distinguish between different types of empathy

- Know that your team isn't your family

Understand how empathy and leadership work together

How do you see your role as a leader? Do you feel you have to be in the trenches with your teams, sleeves rolled up, working alongside them? That isn't what a leader is for.

It's to scan the horizon and set the standards, not to be the first in and last out or to be on everybody's wavelength all of the time. That's being needy, because it's concerned with how people perceive you, not about the impact you have on the business.

Despite that, you want to show commitment and empathy – I get it. However, being empathetic doesn't necessarily mean being the person with a shoulder to cry on; it's creating an environment in which it's possible to struggle and fail and still be supported; an environment in which high-quality work is valued and – crucially – you provide clarity. These are the things that leaders can do to create an empathetic place to work, because they provide the stability upon which teams develop and grow. Your people don't need a friend in you, but they do want to achieve great things in a company that gives them the professional backup they need. It's far better for your business, not to mention your emotional overdraft, if you measure yourself on how well you're achieving that.

A helpful way of seeing this is to think about the difference between personal responsibility and leadership responsibility. An example of the distinction would be that when you're thinking about your own personal responsibility, other people's mistakes are not automatically your problem to manage. But in terms of leadership responsibility, you have a duty to understand those mistakes and help people to navigate past them. Figure 5 lays out the things that are, and are not, part of your personal and your leadership responsibility. Can you see the difference?

Figure 5   The difference between personal responsibility and leadership responsibility.

Distinguish between different types of empathy

The word 'empathy' is often misused, with the result that it's become a noise rather than anything meaningful. The effect of this is to make it feel more burdensome than it should. There's more to empathy than simply understanding someone and expressing it, so it's worth learning about what it really is.

Daniel Goleman, author of the book *Emotional Intelligence*,[30] has come up with three kinds of empathy: cognitive, emotional and compassionate. Cognitive empathy is when

---

[30] Daniel Goleman, *Emotional Intelligence: Why it can matter more than IQ*. Bloomsbury Publishing Ltd (1995).

you put yourself in someone else's shoes to *understand* their situation and the way that they think; this allows you to communicate in a way that's meaningful to them. Emotional empathy is when you *feel* the emotions that the other person is going through; this creates chemistry and rapport. And compassionate empathy is a combination of the two: you *understand* the person and you *feel* their emotions. You care about them and communicate that: 'I care about you; I'll support you; I have your back.'[31]

If you're only cognitively empathetic, you'll find it hard to connect with and have an impact on someone; for instance, you may feel frustrated because you don't understand why they're not resolving their problem themselves. If you're only emotionally empathetic, you'll feel drained by the experience of being 'inside' the person's feelings and won't have the clarity of thinking that you need to help them. If you're compassionately empathetic, however, you'll have the tools to make a difference to them: the mental understanding of their problem, the sensing of their feelings, and the will to make things better. This is the constructive and rewarding kind of empathy that reduces your emotional overdraft, rather than increasing it.

There's also a difference between empathy and sympathy. The latter is when you show concern for someone's misfortune, whereas empathy is when you put yourself fully in their shoes. I work with leaders who are good people and who often want to be nice to their teams. But

---

[31] See Daniel Goleman and Bill George, 'Authenticity and Empathy'. Available at: https://youtu.be/9oQxFUo9zfM [accessed 29 July 2023].

niceness isn't necessarily a helpful thing; it's a behaviour that comes from sympathy rather than empathy, and from a desire to be liked so that they can feel better about themselves. I suggest to them that they be kind, rather than nice. Kindness is a brilliant quality for any leader to have because it's directional and supportive.

Know that your team isn't your family

I've heard quite a few leaders say that their company is like one big family. But is that really the case? Have you ever sacked anyone in your family? Promoted them? Sometimes, you need to make tough decisions about your team; people need to be replaced or to be released, all for the good of the organization. This isn't something that can happen in families. In any case, I'm not sure that the family analogy is a helpful one in a business context. It implies that families are all well balanced and the model to aspire to. Many families are dysfunctional in some way – our literature and TV shows are full of this – exactly because they're not based on high-functioning organizations. In a team, however, people can perform exceptionally well if they're led and managed in the right way.

If you hear yourself talking about your organization as being like a family, it's worth asking why. Is it because you're striving to be empathetic? If so, you'll be putting a lot of effort into a goal that you won't achieve. At some point, you'll have make a decision that would never be acceptable to a member of your family but might be to a member of your team. For instance, you don't like to ask people to stay after 5:30pm. That's okay in general, but if it's the most appropriate thing for the business on a particular day, you need to push for it. Maybe you feel guilty because you've not been organized enough to stop a crisis occurring, or you're worried about losing the affection of your staff, and so you compensate by being nice. These thoughts layer pressure on you and are a great example of why the misuse of empathy can be so damaging for your emotional wellbeing.

The bottom line

- Empathy, when misapplied and misunderstood, can cause you to fail to lead.

- It can also increase your emotional overdraft because you're looking for feelings of acceptance and belonging in the wrong place.

- Addressing this problem involves understanding what empathy really is.

- You also need to learn how leadership and empathy work together, what the different kinds of empathy are and why your business isn't like a family unit.

16
Self-worth

'It makes me feel needed'
'My work is important to me'

WHEN I DID my original research for this book, during which I talked to a variety of leaders about what led them to draw on their emotional reserves rather than do things differently, the concept of self-worth came up again and again. People wanted to feel important and worthwhile in their organizations, and they tended to measure their sense of self-worth through their level of commitment to their teams and the tasks they themselves carried out.

Having a sense of self-worth is, of course, a good thing, but it's rarely the best reason for doing something that increases your emotional overdraft. If you're getting involved in work that you shouldn't be doing because you want your employees to think that you're important and special, you're putting pressure on your resilience. And if you're working too hard or too long because you derive your sense of self from your professional achievements, it's a recipe for burnout.

Often we chase a feeling of self-worth because we think it will make us happy, but there's a tension between success at work and personal happiness. As podcaster Chris Williamson, who's interviewed hundreds of high achievers on his show, says: 'A lot of the time we sacrifice the thing we want for the thing which is supposed to get it. … In service of becoming happy, we sacrifice happiness to achieve success in the hopes that success will make us happy.'[32] This crazy equation manifests itself in the behaviour of founders and leaders who are driven by a fear of insufficiency. Many of us grew up being praised for our successes, which caused us to fear being a loser to the point at which we'll sacrifice our happiness in order to be successful, in the search – ironically – for happiness.

What happens when you derive your self-worth from your work

One of the things that I found interesting about my conversations with people about self-worth was that it highlighted the artificial distinction we make between work and home. Without realizing it, we tend to expect work to give us our sense of self-worth, which we then carry through into our home life. When Anne carried

---

[32] See Chris Williamson, 'The Shocking New Research on Why Men and Women Are No Longer Compatible'. Available at: https://youtu.be/K2tGt2XWd9Q [accessed 29 July 2023].

out her emotional overdraft monitoring, she realized that the temporary difficulties she was having at home were draining her resilience levels. However, she was also topping them up by achieving things that she knew she was good at at work. I think a lot of leaders do the same.

I've always hated the term 'work–life balance' because there's no such thing. There's only life, some of which is spent doing your job and some of which is spent on other things. This makes judging your self-worth through the quality of your work a dangerous thing to do, because in reality it's created across the whole of your life. If you think that it comes mainly from being respected and highly achieving in your job, you're expecting too much of your leadership role and giving your colleagues and clients responsibility for your wellbeing.

It's also an unreliable and inconsistent way to feel good about yourself. It's fine when things are going well – when your profits are up, your team is singing your praises and you've just won a juicy new client. But what happens when you have a bad week? Where does your self-esteem come from then? You've left yourself vulnerable to the ups and downs of business life. And, because your emotional overdraft doesn't get left behind on your desk, it comes home with you and affects the things that you do (and don't do) with the people you care about. Maybe your kids are already in bed by the time you walk through the door; maybe you let your sports team down (again); maybe you haven't read a book in months; maybe you miss dinner with your partner; or maybe you have dinner together and then you open your laptop and do more work. This continues to erode your resilience, and you can't simply expect to top it back up when you go to work; that's a see-saw approach that only causes more stress. Both you and your loved ones are paying the price for your attachment to your work-based sense of self-worth. At some point, your life will start to unravel – your kids will stop confiding in you, your friends will drift away, your relationship will suffer, and you'll become more and more unhealthy and stressed. Is it worth the price?

Mira summed up this vicious cycle beautifully when she said to me, 'You can't pour from an empty cup. Sometimes I'm so overworked that I just want to be by myself when I come home, but then I find myself feeling lonely because I'm not investing time and effort into building friendships and keeping in touch with people. I should be putting more of my energies into the other things that matter to me.' Her emotional overdraft monitoring gave her ideas for resolving these issues, such as shutting her laptop in the evenings and planning ways to flex her work around her children and her love of travel. Just realizing that she had a problem was the first step towards reducing her emotional overdraft.

How to increase your self-worth in constructive ways

Much like with empathy, dealing with the problem of attaching your self-worth to your work involves having some inner realizations. However, there are also practical actions you can take. Here are some approaches:

- Find more constructive ways to feel significant

- Know what you want

- Make yourself redundant in your business

- Recognize your own neediness

Find more constructive ways to feel significant

According to life and business strategist Tony Robbins, there are six basic human needs that we all try to fulfil: certainty, variety, connection, growth, contribution and significance.[33] It's the last of these that I'd like to address here: significance, or feeling unique, important, special or needed. It's only natural to want to matter and if we don't meet our need for significance we can end up behaving in dysfunctional ways. Robbins goes on to explain that there are two approaches to feeling significant: productive and destructive. To me, feeling significant through productive means involves doing rewarding things that strengthen your resilience, such as inspiring your people to do great work. Feeling significant through destructive means involves doing things that give you attention or feed your need for validation, such as putting someone down in a meeting because you want everyone to think you're the smartest person in the room.

What sort of significance are you seeking? And are you looking for it through constructive or destructive means? The destructive route is costly for your emotional overdraft. At the end of your life, nobody will remember how much you earned or how busy you were, but they will remember how you made them feel and whether you spent

---

[33] See Tony Robbins, 'The Human Need for Significance'. Available at: www.tonyrobbins.com/personal-growth/need-for-significance [accessed 29 July 2023].

time with them. Those are the kinds of things that give you significance in the true sense of the word.

Know what you want

Over the years, much of my sense of self-worth has come from hiring great people and bringing out the best in them. I get a kick out of spotting talent and seeing it flourish, and while I've not been perfect at it by any means, I think that it's something I'm good at and enjoy. It's certainly a more constructive route to happiness than trying to be the most important person in the company. When I see people whom I've hired in the past going on to achieve success, it pays back my overdraft again and again. In fact, it's one of the cheapest top-ups I know.

What's your plan to do more of the things that feed your resilience? Do you even know what they are? And how will you incorporate them into your daily life? If you're like many leaders, you may have slipped into doing work that depletes your emotional reserves. Instead of spending your weeks on things you love, you rush from one crisis to the next. Or maybe you'd give anything for the opportunity to learn something new, but when was the last time you did that? How you manage to incorporate more reward into your life is what we'll look at next.

Make yourself redundant in your business

A couple of years ago, I carried out a business planning session with a client, Alexander. He ran a PR company of around 30 people, which had grown quickly and was extremely profitable. While we were still elbow deep in sticking hundreds of Post-it notes across the walls of his conference room, he stopped and leaned on the whiteboard. I'll never forget what he said next: 'You know what, Andy? My dream would be to take a month off.' I looked at him for a moment and then replied, 'Well, let's do it then. Let's build your holiday into the plan. At the moment, I don't think your business is independent enough of you for you to be able to take four weeks off, but if you make the right changes you can have that holiday as soon as next year.'

So he did. The following summer, after taking steps to ensure that he could leave the office for four weeks, he took off on a trip with his family. This was only possible because he'd worked hard to dissociate his sense of self-worth from being present in the business. He was a bit nervous before he went, but he had a brilliant time. There was a double benefit: he reduced his company's dependence on him, and he boosted his resilience. Prior to this, Alexander had been a classic workaholic. He rarely saw his family, interfered in every aspect of the business and was a case study of someone living in a permanent emotional overdraft. He genuinely thought that he had to be the best at everything: the best writer, the best strategist, the best networker. But through his own effort and determination, and with a bit of coaching and support from people around him, he started to realize that he could have a different life. He made slightly less profit than usual that year, but he stopped subsidizing his company through his emotional overdraft and recognized what he needed to do if he was to have a sustainable approach to running it. I was delighted for him, so much so that I'm thinking of doing the same thing myself.

Have a think about how this relates to you. If I was to suggest that you took a month off, could you contemplate the idea? Would you trust your business to survive without you, or would you assume that there's no way you could ever have that luxury? And it needn't be a vacation; imagine if you were hospitalized and not able to contribute for a month. The bottom line is, if your organization would crumble without you being in it for a few weeks, it's overly dependent on you. For Alexander, being the best at everything was not a good thing; not only was it impossible, he was also putting limits on his business's growth.

Whenever I encourage leaders and founders to make themselves redundant in their businesses, I tend to get one of two reactions. One is: 'Oh, that would be great. How do I do it?' The other is: 'What are you talking about? I can't do that!' But remember, roles become redundant, not people. If you find the idea of your role not being needed anymore a frightening one, it's a clue that your self-worth is overly bound up in your work. When you build your company so that it can run without you, it means that you can spend time on the tasks you love, not the stuff that you've fallen into over the years. It's also the ultimate measure of successful leadership.

To do this, you need to define your role and how it differs from those of others in your organization. It's surprisingly rare for founders and leaders to have role descriptions, so, if that's the case for you, make it your next task. As part of the process, you can work out what responsibilities to remove in order to make the company less dependent on you. This will kick-start a process that I've seen work time and again, where a leader takes onerous and irrelevant tasks off their plate and then, suddenly, they can take a month-long holiday.

The irony is that if you make yourself redundant, you'll always have a job. Once you've achieved the goal of enabling your people to excel without you, your responsibility is then to see over the horizon, push the boundaries and encourage them to be innovative. How beneficial would it be for your emotional overdraft if all you had to worry about was that?

Recognize your own neediness

Nobody likes to be thought of as needy, so it might be revealing if you were to ask yourself the following questions:

Do I sign off all expenditure in my business, however minor?

Does it matter to me to be in charge of everything?

If someone proved to me that I was wrong about something, would I feel upset?

Do I feel good when people ask my opinions about things?

It's an awful lot easier than you think to be needy, and it's a great way of increasing your emotional overdraft because not only does being needy put a huge amount of pressure on you to be right about everything, it also takes away your team's ability to make independent judgements. As Dan Rockwell of *Leadership Freak* puts it, 'The more essential you are, the less effective you've become. Tugging toddler-followers may make you feel important, but you aren't – you're needy.'[34] The answer, he explains, is first to recognize your neediness; the more clearly you see it, the better you'll be able to tackle it. Then, develop systems and structures that free people up to do their best work so that you're enabling more and controlling less. You can even smile to yourself when you sense that your neediness is bubbling up – it's quite funny, when you think about it. In time, you'll find that the less you want to feel in control, the more support rises up around you and the easier your working life will be.

The bottom line

- A misunderstanding of where self-worth comes from can lead you to be a person who seeks reassurance rather than leads with confidence.

- When your self-esteem is bound up in your business, you're liable to overwork and neglect other important areas of your life, leading to an increase in your emotional overdraft.

- Inner ways of addressing this problem are finding constructive ways to feel significant and recognizing your own neediness.

- Practical methods are having goals for what you want and enabling your company to run without you being in control of everything.

---

[34] See Dan Rockwell, 'Needy Leaders', *Leadership Freak*, 25 January (2013). Available at: https://leadershipfreak.blog/2013/01/25/needy-leaders/ [accessed 29 July 2023].

Part Four
Taking it One Step Further

17

Creating and Maintaining New Habits

EMOTIONS ARE DESIGNED to be hard to ignore. That's because their purpose is to prompt us to take action – action that will keep us safe. On top of that, we humans are complicated beasts with big brains, and we're often beset by conflicting emotions at the same time. This can make it confusing when we're trying to develop new habits, because what feels good in the moment isn't necessarily what serves our best interests in the long term. That sweet feeling of relief when you step in and blast through a task that someone else should have been handling gives you the impression that you've done the right thing, but what you've really achieved is to reinforce a lifelong habit of JFDI that's compounding your emotional overdraft. This is why behaviour is always the last thing to change. There are many books about how to change (and keep new) habits, but they don't cover how to shift the way you think and work specifically in relation to your emotional overdraft. That's what I'll explore in this chapter.

Let's remind ourselves about where our feelings come from. They derive from our thinking, which in turn drives our emotions, which instigate behaviours, which create outcomes. When you remind yourself that an emotion is only the physical sensation of a thought, it can lose some of its power, because you come to realize that it's your own mind that's generating the feeling rather than what's outside of you. It might not seem like it, but that's the way it works. Taking my example of stepping in to do other people's work, it appears that the circumstances dictate you must take action. However, what's really going on is that your ingrained thought habits are telling you it's imperative to step in, and when you do, you have a good feeling. There are different thoughts that you might have had, such as 'let's see if someone else can handle this', or 'it would be better to find out why this occurred'. In the short term, these thoughts will produce uncomfortable feelings because they're not familiar, but in time they will pay dividends.

It's also worth bearing in mind that reducing your emotional overdraft mainly involves stopping doing stuff that's unhelpful. There's nothing new to learn or get your head around; it's simply a matter of seeing things in a different way. The more inquisitive you are about the process, the easier and more straightforward it will be. It won't happen in an instant because changing behaviour is never quick, but you'll find that the positive impact on your resilience and wellbeing is exponential. Just as behaviours that load more stress onto you can snowball into overwhelm, so those that take away the stress and give you more joy in your work have a cumulative effect. As rapidly as an emotional overdraft can build up, so it can reduce.

How to turn new habits into permanent change

Here are some practical ways that you can develop and keep new habits that will reduce your emotional overdraft:

- Don't boil the ocean

- Go back to your monitoring system

- Bring your monitoring into your management information

- Share the idea

- Be held to account

- Appoint a coach or an adviser

- Plan to relapse

Don't boil the ocean

One of my clients uses this phrase when I start getting a bit too ambitious on his behalf. He means that I'm trying to do too much in one go. So instead of boiling the ocean, limit yourself to a cup of water to start with, because you can't tackle everything at once. Start with returning to the self-assessment process that you went through in Chapter 2. What are the drivers that have the biggest impact on your emotional overdraft? And which ones are less important? Be deliberate about the drivers to focus on.

There are two options when you're thinking about where to begin. You can either choose the driver that's your biggest challenge and work on that, the logic being that if you can improve that one it will have the most significant effect on your emotional overdraft. Or you can start with the driver that seems easiest to change – the quickest win. This will give you a head start and give you the confidence to explore some of the others later.

And what if no particular driver stands out to you? Try looking at the diagram of the 10 drivers (Figure 6), which you first came across in Chapter 2 but is repeated here for convenience. I've grouped them according to the ones that, in my experience, tend to fit most closely together.

Towards the top of the circle is 'At a loss'; if you frequently find it hard to come up with fresh ideas, you could start there. Moving in a clockwise direction, we come to 'Load-balancing', 'Expectation' and 'Duty' – these are frequent stumbling blocks for leaders who have a strong sense of obligation to their businesses. After that are 'Self-worth' and 'Empathy' – these can be a particular challenge for people who identify emotionally with their work. And, finally, we come to 'Trust', 'JFDI', 'Urgency' and 'Cost' – these are often the most significant issues for leaders who find it hard to relinquish control. Of course, there's nothing to say that your own issues are clustered together like this – you can treat the whole diagram as a pick and mix if you like. But you might also find it helpful to see the drivers in groups.

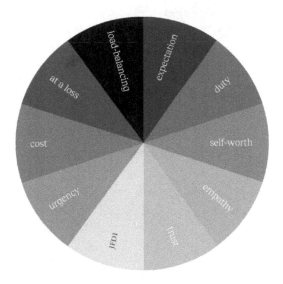

Figure 6   The emotional overdraft drivers reviewed

Go back to your monitoring system

Remember Chapter 5, where I talked you through creating a monitoring system for your emotional overdraft? Did you start doing it then? If so great, but, if not, this is the time to get it going. I appreciate that the last thing you need when you're busy is for me to give you something else to do, but I had a good reason for asking you to carry out this exercise: you can't change what you don't understand.

The benefit of the monitoring is that the results are hard to ignore because they're factual. Don't assume that you'll remember events accurately if you cast your mind back over the past month; like all people, you have a recency bias, which means that you give greater weight to events that happened yesterday than those that happened two weeks ago. You need to do the monitoring every day, if only for a month (and you can carry on longer if you want).

Another reason for carrying out the monitoring is that you can see patterns emerging, which will help you to decide what drivers to start with. You may even find that your behaviour will start to shift while you're doing the monitoring; I've seen this happen with the leaders I work with time and again. It's almost ridiculous how impactful it is just to be aware of what's draining your resilience and what's boosting it before you even think consciously about changing anything.

Bring your monitoring into your management information

Management information is intelligence that you can use in your business to make better decisions. Would knowing if your emotional overdraft has increased or decreased in a particular month be a useful piece of data to have? I think it would. When you do this, you're revealing the invisible cost line in your company's P&L that I talked about at the beginning of the book: the personal subsidy that you're providing to your business in order to increase its financial profits.

I'm a great believer in using figures to show your direction of travel, rather than treating them in isolation. For instance, if you start with an index of 100 for your emotional overdraft and the following month it rises to 109, that might not in itself say much. But if the month after it tracks at 128, then a month after that it falls to 115, that's telling you something you need to know. What happened during that time that caused it to rise and fall? You need to understand this just as much as what triggered your business's revenue and profits to change.

You may be wondering how you would include your emotional overdraft figures in your management information when they're only for you and not for the rest of your team. This is something that we'll cover in the next chapter, but for now you can start thinking about how making your level of wellbeing visible in this way would be helpful as a prompt for examining your habits.

Share the idea

Linked to the notion of including your emotional overdraft monitoring in your management information is that of sharing the concept of an emotional overdraft with other people. The benefit of this is that you'll gain support, because when they understand what you're trying to achieve and have a common language with which to talk to you about it, they'll be in a stronger position to help you. The people you share it with could be friends, colleagues or members of your family – anyone who has an interest in your wellbeing.

Don't be shy – having an emotional overdraft is something that every single leader experiences. My research proves that. All you're doing by talking about it is giving a name to something that already exists and showing that you want to do something about it. If any of your colleagues feel inspired by the idea and want to make changes for themselves, you can even share notes. Just bear in mind that everyone's resilience levels are different and that, while it's helpful to compare their findings with yours, you shouldn't feel as if you're in competition.

Be held to account

I'll be honest, I spent two years thinking about writing this book before I made any concrete progress. What kickstarted me was when I went on to LinkedIn and posted this update: 'I'm writing a book and I want to have it finished by this summer. Please ask me how I'm getting on – I need the accountability.' I also told my clients about it and those in my network outside of LinkedIn. Now I have a group of people who are regularly asking me how the book is going and when it's coming out. They're even wanting to review and contribute to it.

In the same way, I encourage you to ask the people you trust to hold you to account with the changes you're making to your habitual behaviour. Tell them that you're monitoring the changes and that you'll show your numbers to them, about what it's doing going through and encourage them to be involved and interested. It's important to create a structure, so put dates in the diary to update people. Be brave with this; it's not easy to open up or feel vulnerable, but that's why it's such a powerful experience. Also, I can guarantee you that everyone will relate to the concept of an emotional overdraft and want to share in your journey.

Who can you ask for accountability? Do you have a mentor on your personal board, or a coach, or someone you can rely on to be honest with you? You could share your first month's monitoring results with them and they could tell you what they think. Also, by exploring your analysis with the other person, they may give you insights that you'd never have come up with on your own.

One final point about accountability: you need to give people permission to call you out if your behaviour lapses into its old ways, and also not to give them a hard time if they do. They may have spent a long time learning to keep quiet when they see you feeling stressed or angry because it makes your mood worse. So, if they say something like, 'You're getting uptight because you're trying to do everything yourself,' don't snap at them – thank them instead.

Appoint a coach or an adviser

It took me a long time to realize that I would benefit from coaching, not because I didn't think I had anything to learn but because I didn't understand what it was. Here's how coaching works. A coach will challenge you, ask you questions about why you do certain things or think a certain way, and support you in finding new ways of working. Through this, they'll help you to re-examine the self-image you've unconsciously cultivated through years of practice. This is important because, as James Clear explains in his book *Atomic Habits*, 'On any given day, you may struggle with your habits because you're too busy or too tired or too overwhelmed or hundreds of other reasons. Over the long run, however, the real reason you fail to stick with habits is that your self-image gets in the way. This is why you can't get too attached to one version of your identity.'[35] Coaching can be a game changer when it comes to seeing yourself in a new light, creating different habits and embedding them in your working life.

I also encourage you to find an adviser. The existence of business advisers seems to be a well-kept secret – I didn't know about them myself until 10 years ago – but it's a resource that can be of great use. An adviser is a person who will help you make better business decisions more quickly than you'd have done on your own. They'll encourage you, support you and hold you to account. Unlike a coach, who can (and often should) be outside of your industry, it's best if an adviser has experience of the kind of work you do. This means that they'll be able to anticipate some of the challenges you face and act as a sounding board for any issues you want to discuss. I work as an adviser for various companies and have often been described as a knowledgeable older brother, something I take as a huge compliment; it describes the kind of relationship it should be.

Plan to relapse

It's incredibly hard to shift deep-rooted ways of behaving; ask anyone who's been on a diet if they've managed to keep it up long term. So, it makes sense to assume that at some point you'll relapse into not trusting people, acting out of duty, over-empathizing, or whatever driver happens to be your personal bugbear.

---

[35] James Clear, *Atomic Habits: An Easy and Proven Way to Build Good Habits and Break Bad Ones*, Random House Business Books (2018), p. 36.

First, become aware of what's happening. This is where your support network can help, because they already know about your challenges and are quite likely on the receiving end of them when you slip back into your old ways. Then, instead of giving yourself a hard time or being horribly judgemental about your slip-up, get curious. There was no failure involved, it was only you pushing the boundaries of what you felt comfortable with. What triggered the relapse? What was going on for you at the time? And what can you learn from it?

Whatever you do, don't give up. Relapsing in the context of an emotional overdraft is actually as serious as relapsing with smoking or drinking, even if it's not as obvious. So just start again – there's no prize for continuity but there is for concerted effort. If you get a flat tyre, do you junk your whole car instead of just replacing the wheel? That would be ridiculous, right? But it's often how we think about 'failure' when we try to achieve something and fall by the wayside. Lapsing and plateauing are a normal; they don't mean we should call it a day.

There's another powerful tool that you can create to cater for future lapses, which is to assemble what I call a relapse kit. Let's assume that empathy is one of your key drivers for an emotional overdraft, and that one day you notice your stress levels are rising because you're working late alongside your staff yet again. What have you prepared for when that moment happens? You might have written a note and put it in your desk drawer to remind yourself of the downsides of misapplied empathy. The note could also contain advice about what to do, such as to speak to your coach or to walk away from the situation temporarily –

whatever works for you. You could even ask your support network to sign that note ahead of time and to act as a sounding board when the time comes. Other options are to create a document that you save onto your desktop with some articles that you found useful when you were first exploring the issue. Or there could be pictures of your family which remind you about why you're doing this in the first place – to spend more time with them. The point is that you know this is going to happen and you're prepared for it. This gives you a way of controlling the situation and seeing a way forward, which in itself will reduce your emotional overdraft. Instead of feeling stuck, you have an oven-ready solution.

The bottom line

- Changing your behaviour is hard to keep up long term, so you need strategies.

- It's helpful to remember that your emotions come from your thinking, not from your circumstances.

- Choose which driver to work on first and make use of your monitoring data, working it into your management information.

- Share what you're trying to achieve with others and ask them to hold you to account.

- Plan to relapse, so that when you do, you have a recovery kit set up.

18
Team Emotional Overdraft

Y OU'RE NOT THE only person in your organization with an emotional overdraft. Given how pervasive the issue is, you can be sure that everyone in your senior leadership team is also in emotional deficit, so it makes sense to look at it from a team perspective. Apart from anything else, the great month you've just had might have been at the expense of someone else's resilience levels. An emotional overdraft always finds somewhere to live, so unless each member of your team is changing their behaviour, it will tend to hang out in someone else's head.

When you think about the negative impact everyone's emotional overdrafts are having, not only on their wellbeing but also on the way the company is run, it makes even more sense to see it as a collective movement and not just as your own personal issue. I've been on the boards of various businesses for 25 years, and I can see now that if we'd all known about this issue at the time, we would have made far better decisions. Certainly, we'd have made them more quickly than we did at the time.

There's also the multiplier effect to take into account. You could carry on seeing the reduction of your own emotional overdraft as a personal mission, and given your position in the organization, it would have a ripple effect for sure. But imagine how much you could increase that if every senior person in your company was to go through the same process as you. How much wider would those ripples spread? If all the members of your leadership team saw the size of their emotional overdrafts as indicators of how well or badly they were managing the business, they would automatically look at ways of re-engineering what they do. Not only that, but their resilience levels would also be higher, which would lead them to be more effective problem solvers and better people to work for.

An additional benefit to embedding this thinking into your senior team is that it gives you a shared language with which to talk about the emotional overdraft. This allows you to support each other, further increasing the multiplier effect. When you're looking at everyone's emotional overdrafts in your management information each month, you can all understand it and have an input. It might be that specific areas of the business are struggling more than others, for instance, and that with the objectivity given by distance, individual leaders can help each other to remove the interference that causes 'stuck' and unhelpful behaviours. In this way, you're creating a sustainable, successful business that's easier to run than the one you have now.

How to embed change in your senior leadership team

The first step is to share the understanding that you've gained about your emotional overdraft with the key people in your organization. You can even lend them a copy of this book if you like. Afterwards, there are three simple ways in which you can embed new ways of behaving in your senior team:

- Collect and use the data

- Talk about it

- Support each other

Collect and use the data

In a business that I once ran that was owned by another company, we had an incredibly successful year in terms of both growth and profitability. The reason for the growth was extra clients, which was of course good news, but the reason for the profitability was that we struggled to recruit enough quality people to cope with the increased workload. My hugely motivated team took this on themselves, and we managed to eke out an extra 25% of revenue without hiring anyone new. This was followed by another equally successful year, by which point the team was creaking at the seams. I told the board of our parent company that we could continue to grow but that we'd been borrowing against the resilience of my team for too long; if we carried on like this, we'd either damage our people or lose them. The last thing I wanted was to get into a vicious cycle where my best people drifted off, the worst stayed and the business went slowly downhill until it collapsed. The board's response was that shareholder satisfaction was all they cared about, with the result that I ended up leaving the business. It was a huge shame that, at the time, I didn't have that missing piece of data: the emotional overdraft figure. If I had, I could have made different decisions that might have avoided my impasse with the board.

To ensure that you have the right data, ask everyone to monitor their emotional overdrafts in the same way as you have, just for a month (as outlined in Chapter 5). Then see what the results are and discuss including them in your management information reviews going forward. The key benefit of management information is that it's intelligence you can use to help the business make better decisions. If you don't include your (or your leadership team's) emotional overdraft in this information, you're missing a key data point that will tell you what levers to pull in order to impact the long-term sustainability of your company. You're continuing to keep the invisible cost line in the P&L – the one that represents the way that you're all subsidizing the profitability of the company with your personal resilience – hidden.

If your senior team is in agreement, I suggest that you all carry out the monitoring each month, then aggregate the figures for the whole team and see whether they rise or fall. There's often a tendency with management information to have too much detail, whereas what you want is a clear summary with some critical figures. When you put the leadership team's overall emotional overdraft figure on the dashboard, it ensures that it receives the same attention as your total marketing or salary spend.

Talk about it

When you have the facts in front of you, you can start to talk about what needs to change if the emotional overdraft has increased (or, indeed, how you're going to celebrate if it's reduced). You're looking for common or recurring themes, or behaviours that have had a significant impact on people's resilience levels.

For instance, you might have won a new client and, in order to handle the extra workload, put off some important strategic planning time; this has had a negative impact on some of the senior team who were relying on you delivering the plan. Instead of shrugging this off as 'one of those things that happens when you win a new client' as you might have done in the past, you can now look at it differently. What does it say about your company's recruitment processes, or the way that you manage your staff? Why did this happen? Could it have been handled differently? Management intelligence is of no use unless you see it as a lever to make your business work more effectively.

Support each other

Once you've extended the idea of the emotional overdraft from yourself to your leadership team, it seems like the natural next step to support each other with it. Expecting people to identify and fix their drivers on their own isn't realistic, and there may be all sorts of ways that you can help each other, whether it be by acting as a sounding board or suggesting more training.

This is where the power of diverse thinking comes in. I'm currently working with the members of a senior leadership team who have identified that out of the 10 drivers of an emotional overdraft, they each have different combinations of behaviours that need to be addressed. They also, however, have different strengths. One person doesn't find trust to be an issue and is great at delegating, while another finds it easy to hold back from JFDI-ing. They've now paired up so that they can support each other in the areas that their counterpart finds most difficult. It's a fascinating dynamic because they've gone from being a loose group of people working in a fractured way, each leader running their own department and not communicating much with the others, to a cohesive team whose members have empathy for one another and are helping themselves to grow and change. This is having an immediate impact on the running of the business as well as on the resilience levels of the entire group.

Being open about your vulnerabilities and shortcomings, and helping others with theirs, is hugely bonding, especially if you don't normally work closely with your colleagues. You're getting to know each other on a whole new level, which can be rewarding in its own right. Also, by enabling the removal of barriers to emotional wellbeing and business success, you're accelerating the process of improvement – it's like you've put it on steroids.

The bottom line

- Embedding an understanding of the emotional overdraft into your senior leadership team has several benefits: it multiplies and accelerates the positive impact on the business, it strengthens the team's resilience and it allows team members to support each other.

- Putting this into practice starts with ensuring that everyone is monitoring their emotional overdrafts and making the results visible.

- It continues with discussions about how to reduce the collective emotional overdraft, and instituting ways of helping each other to reduce it.

Conclusion

I'M SURE THAT by this stage you've spotted the hidden benefit in reducing your emotional overdraft: that by paying attention to your personal wellbeing, you're also uncovering the things that you need to improve in your business. Before, your emotionally costly behaviour was masking them. You leapt in to do things yourself, which meant that your staff didn't have the chance to develop. You took on the extra workload when you won a new client, which meant that your business never benefited from the planning that should have happened. Or you weren't sure about where your role ended and other people's began, which meant that nobody else was clear about what they were doing either. It's a game changer when you realize that trying less hard to run your business can also make it more successful.

There are some action-based themes that you may have noticed coming up again and again throughout the book, so it's worth summarizing them here.

Design an organizational structure

Having a flat, informal structure is fine when you're starting up, but when you hire more people you need an organization chart. If your business doesn't have a clear structure, you end up doing other people's jobs because you're not sure what your own job is. This is a recipe for overwork for you, and one for frustration and inefficiency for other people. When you've put in place a sound structure, however, everyone knows where they stand. Not only that, but it's a liberator for your business because you have solid foundations on which to grow.

Create role descriptions for everyone, including yourself

Linked to clarity of structure is clarity of roles. This is integral to you knowing what you should and shouldn't be doing, and the beauty of having role descriptions is that not only do they encourage you to draw firmer boundaries, they also help you to focus on the kind of work that's of most value. You'll find it far more rewarding to go home each day knowing that you've focused on what only you can do, rather than on what other people can accomplish themselves.

Delegate

When you have a structure and clear roles, it gives you the basis from which to delegate. That means you don't run yourself ragged and at the same time demotivate and deskill the people who work for you. It's also important to delegate consistently and well, so that people understand what they're being asked to do and by when.

Be accountable

A structure and role descriptions will give you a framework to work more efficiently, but without being held accountable you might slip into your old habits. It's helpful to have around you people who can point out when that's happening, and also to formalize your accountability so that you're being appraised in the same way as your staff.

Get to know yourself

A large part of how much headway you make with reducing your emotional overdraft is down to how open you are to learning about the mental barriers that you've innocently put in your own way. There's probably little in Part Three of this book that you didn't know already, but the problem is that you haven't been seeing it or taking action on it. Once you know the drivers that are causing you to sabotage your own efforts, the path forward becomes clear.

Understand what real leadership is

Being a leader isn't being a dictator; nor (conversely) is it being the nice guy or the friend. It's being the person who sets a clear direction for your team and inspires them to work towards it. In order to know what that direction is, you have to think strategically and make plans; these will be a lot easier for you to create when you're not trying to do everything else at the same time. Once everyone in the business has something to aim at, many of your problems will fall away.

Above all, I encourage you to make a start on reducing your emotional overdraft right now. Bring your own perspective to the process, have honest conversations with yourself and, if you think you'd find it helpful, open up those conversations to other people. There's always a way to re-frame a problem or to do something differently. As Mira said to me, 'I've realized that there's no point in building a great business. I should be focusing on building a great life.' She's right, and what I'll add to her wise words is that a great business can be a consequence of a great life, because of the extra resilience you have when you're not sinking under the weight of your emotional overdraft.

You don't have to have an emotional overdraft just because you're a leader. There are so many ways in which you can reduce or eliminate it. Even if you take action on just one of the drivers, you'll be making a significant difference. You'll be starting a journey that ends with you feeling happier, cultivating better work and personal relationships, and – as an incredible added bonus – a more vibrant and rewarding business.

The Author

THIRTY-FIVE YEARS AGO, Andy Brown paid his way through college by carrying out street interviews for advertising agencies. This taught him not to be shy and also got him hooked on advertising. Since then, he's run various creative businesses, some for others and some for himself. Most were made up of 50–80 people (companies the government rather sniffily refers to as SMEs), and he quickly learnt that businesses that depend on people for their success need to be led in a way that makes them sustainable.

For the past seven years, he's worked as an adviser and coach for people-based businesses, some as small as a five-man band and some as substantial as the M&C Saatchi group. As well as winning Outstanding Non-Executive Director of the Year in 2021, he's helped his clients to increase their company value – because valuable businesses have more opportunity to make an impact. He's done this by enabling founders and leaders to 'make better decisions, more quickly', as one client put it.

He's a hybrid of a benign older sibling, an encouraging parent, an experienced friend and a coach, and his clients tell him that they value being with him on their journey. Many of them have managed to sustain a profit growth of between 20% and 50%, while reducing their emotional overdrafts at the same time.

You can find out more about Andy's advisory work and his work with leaders at www.andybrown.coach. If you'd like access to resources related to this book, head over to www. emotionaloverdraft.com.

Acknowledgements

THIS IS NOT my book, it's a collection of stories about people I've met and worked with over the years. Thank you to everyone who shared their ideas and helped me to develop the emotional overdraft concept, even if you didn't know you were doing it at the time. In recent years, I've been lucky enough to work with some clients who've also been generous enough to allow me to explore these ideas with my readers. The way that you approach your challenges and opportunities is an inspiration every day. Thank you.

I'd like to name check a few people who have specifically helped me with the book.

Particular thanks to my 'guinea pigs': Billy Johnson, Caroline Till, Hana Clode and Sarah Jennings. You were generous enough to let me dig deeper into some of my ideas – and your lives!

Thank you to Darren Lassiter, Nick Farrar, Kirstie Smith, Luke Brynley-Jones and Paul Williams for helping me test the models.

To those of you who made time to help me with the original research, I'll always be grateful. I know how hard it is to find the capacity to add one more thing to your to-do list. Thank you to Sam Page, Cheryl Thomas, Ed Burnand, Nick Dudley-Williams, Ed Gossage, Neil Collard, George Owen, John Onion, Twink Field, David Hordle, Andy Hayes, Richard Temple, Andrew Scott, Mike Spurling, Stef Lait, Luther Spicer, Trenton Moss, Ruth Johnson, Paul O'Malley, Laura Daniel, Nikki Fraser, Naomi Goodman and Camilla Honey.

Having mentioned it in the book, I should call out my personal board. Thanks to David Batten, my cheerleader; Bruce O'Brien, my coach; Dan Moore, my peer; David Welling, my long-time mentor; and Derek Clark, my wellness coach.

I wouldn't have got the book started without the support of my one and only colleague, Amy Greenwood. And without doubt, this book would not have seen the light of day if it hadn't have been for the incredible energy, experience, persistence and tenacity of my editor, the rockstar Ginny Carter.

Lastly, I want to thank Beverley, my wife and life partner. I'll never be able to repay the faith and confidence you have in me, but I'll keep trying.

Index

A quick word from Practical Inspiration Publishing...

We hope you found this book both practical and inspiring – that's what we aim for with every book we publish.

We publish titles on topics ranging from leadership, entrepreneurship, HR and marketing to self-development and wellbeing.

Find details of all our books at: www.practicalinspiration.com

 Did you know...

We can offer discounts on bulk sales of all our titles – ideal if you want to use them for training purposes, corporate giveaways or simply because you feel these ideas deserve to be shared with your network.

We can even produce bespoke versions of our books, for example with your organization's logo and/or a tailored foreword.

To discuss further, contact us on info@practicalinspiration.com.

 Got an idea for a business book?

We may be able to help. Find out more about publishing in partnership with us at: bit.ly/PIpublishing.

Follow us on social media...

@PIPTalking

@pip_talking

@practicalinspiration

@piptalking

Practical Inspiration Publishing